natural English

pre-intermediate workbook with key

Lyn Scott & David Scott

OXFORD

UNIVERSITY PRESS

contents

3

Tick (✓) when you've done these sections.

natural English
- [ ] *What's ... like?*
- [ ] showing a lot of interest
- [ ] possessive *'s*
- [ ] *both*

grammar
- [ ] question forms
- [ ] past simple
- [ ] expand your grammar *neither*

vocabulary
- [ ] talking about you and your family
- [ ] relatives
- [ ] expand your vocabulary describing things

how to ask questions

natural English *What's ... like?*

1   Match the questions and answers.

- [e]   What's the <u>house</u> like?
- 1 [ ]   What's the <u>weather</u> like?
- 2 [ ]   What was the <u>film</u> like?
- 3 [ ]   What's your <u>sister</u> like?
- 4 [ ]   What was the <u>food</u> like?
- 5 [ ]   What was the <u>party</u> like?
- 6 [ ]   What's your <u>teacher</u> like?
- 7 [ ]   What's the <u>beach</u> like?
- 8 [ ]   What's their <u>new CD</u> like?

a   Great. There were lots of people there.

b   A bit boring, actually. It was too long and Julia Roberts wasn't very good.

c   The dessert was fantastic.

d   Some of the songs on it are great.

e   ~~Really big inside with a beautiful garden~~.

f   Really cold. We get a lot of snow at this time of the year.

g   Beautiful, and the water is really clear.

h   Good. I like his classes.

i   Actually, she's a bit shy and quiet. Not like me at all!

say it!

pronunciation Notice the stressed words (<u>underlined</u>) in exercise 1. Practise asking the questions.

You meet someone from New Zealand. Ask them questions about ...

the weather	their town
the countryside	the people
the food	

> What's the <u>weather</u> like?

Now answer the questions about your own country.

expand your vocabulary

describing things

Here are more answers for questions 1 to 8 in exercise 1. What / who is being described?

~~a person~~	a film	a hotel
the weather	a party	some food
a book	a CD	a teacher

She's very **sociable**. /ˈsəʊʃəbl/ _a person_

1 It was very **scary** /ˈskeəri/ and Brad Pitt was good in it. _____

2 It was very **luxurious**. /lʌɡˈʒʊəriəs/ _____

3 It's often very **humid**. _____

4 It was **fun** and I met lots of people. _____

5 The story's really **complicated**. /ˈkɒmplɪkeɪtɪd/ _____

6 The first song is very **catchy**. _____

7 It's a bit too **spicy** for me. _____

8 He's **popular** with all the students. _____

Read sentences 1 to 8 again and match the words in bold with definitions a to h.

likes going out and meeting people _sociable_

a very comfortable and expensive _____

b enjoyable _____

c frightening _____

d has a lot of chilli in it _____

e the air is warm and wet _____

f you hear it once and remember it _____

g lots of people like him _____

h difficult to understand _____

test yourself!

Read definitions **a** to **h** again and cover the answers. Remember the adjectives.

grammar question forms

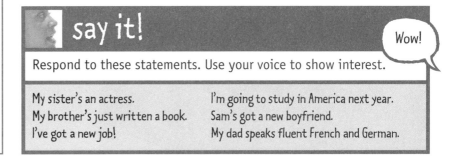

2 Samantha is on a train in Italy. She's reading an English magazine. Gabriela is Italian. Write her questions.

G Excuse me, _are you from England_ ? (from England)

S Yes, I am.

G ¹_____ ? (What / name)

S I'm Samantha.

G ²_____ ? (Where / live)

S In London.

G I like London. ³_____ ? (What / do there)

S I'm a photographer.

G That's interesting! ⁴_____ ? (on holiday / Italy)

S Yes, I'm visiting my brother. He lives here with his wife.

G Really! ⁵_____ ? (she / Italian)

S Yes, she is.

G ⁶_____ ? (Where / meet)

S In Italy when he was studying Italian. She was his teacher!

G Wow! ⁷_____ ? (Have got / children)

S Yes, a little boy.

G ⁸_____ ? (How old)

S Thomas is four.

G ⁹_____ ? (How often / brother / go back to England)

S Two or three times every year. He works for an airline so he travels for free.

G That's fantastic!

natural English showing a lot of interest

3 In exercise 2 underline four phrases that Gabriela uses to show interest.

say it!

Respond to these statements. Use your voice to show interest.

Wow!

My sister's an actress.	I'm going to study in America next year.
My brother's just written a book.	Sam's got a new boyfriend.
I've got a new job!	My dad speaks fluent French and German.

wordbooster

talking about you and your family

think back!

Remember five words for people in your family.   *sister*

4 Make new sentences with the same meaning. Use the words given.

Every Christmas my relatives get together.   celebration
Every Christmas *we have a big family celebration.*

1 I haven't got any brothers or sisters.   only
   I _____

2 I don't live with anyone else.   own
   I _____

3 We often have arguments.   a lot
   We _____

4 I have a good relationship with my boss.   get on
   I _____

5 The teachers at school have a lot of rules.   strict
   The teachers _____

6 My sister looks after her child alone.   parent
   My sister _____

7 Their wedding was last September.   married
   They _____

8 My brother and I have a good relationship.   close
   My brother and I _____

relatives

5 Who are Lynda's relatives? Replace the underlined words with a word from the box.

~~grandfather~~	daughter	aunt	nephew
brother-in-law	cousin	niece	uncle
stepfather			

Edward was her <u>mum's father</u>.
grandfather _____

1 John is her <u>sister's husband</u>.
   _____

2 Katie's her <u>brother's daughter</u>.
   _____

3 David's her <u>mum's brother</u>.
   _____

4 Jenny's her <u>mum's sister</u>.
   _____

5 Luke's her <u>brother's son</u>.
   _____

6 Peter's her <u>mum's second husband</u>.
   _____

7 Anna's her <u>uncle's child</u>.
   _____

8 Isabella's her <u>baby girl</u>.
   _____

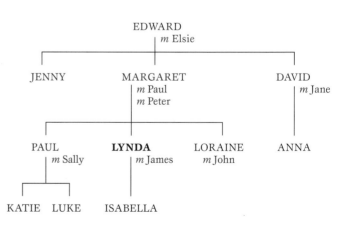

EDWARD
m Elsie

JENNY   MARGARET   DAVID
               m Paul   *m* Jane
               m Peter

PAUL   **LYNDA**   LORAINE   ANNA
m Sally   *m* James   *m* John

KATIE   LUKE   ISABELLA

relationships

natural English possessive 's

6 Look at the family tree on *p.6*. Answer the questions. More than one answer may be possible.

	Who's Sally?	She's	*Paul's*	wife.
1	Who's John?	He's	_____	husband.
2	Who's James?	He's	_____	father.
3	Who's Jane?	She's	_____	mother.
4	Who's Luke?	He's	_____	son.
5	Who's Elsie?	She's	_____	grandmother.
6	Who's Katie?	She's	_____	sister.
7	Who's Sally?	She's	_____	sister-in-law.
8	Who's Loraine?	She's	_____	aunt.

test yourself!

Look at the family tree again and talk about the people.

Sally is Paul's wife. Sally is Lynda's sister-in-law.

grammar past simple

7 Complete the article using verbs from the box in the past simple.

| get | start | have | sit | rent | be | leave | do | ~~meet~~ | talk | move |

friends...

I _met_ my best friend Kate on our first day at school 15 years ago. We ^{1}_____ a new school on the same day. We ^{2}_____ next to each other in class every day and we ^{3}_____ on the phone every evening. In fact, we ^{4}_____ everything together. When we were sixteen we even ^{5}_____ jobs in the same shop on Saturdays.

Me and Kate 1993

When we ^{6}_____ school we chose the same university in London and we ^{7}_____ a flat together. It ^{8}_____ terrible. I'm really tidy and she's messy. She loves loud music whereas I'm quieter. After two days in the same house we ^{9}_____ our first argument! After three months she ^{10}_____ out. We're still best friends but we never lived together again!

grammar past simple
question forms and negatives

8 Complete the sentences using the words given.

	A	What _did you do_ (do) last night?
	B	I watched TV.
1	A	What was the restaurant like yesterday?
	B	We _____ (not / go). We got a **takeaway** instead.
2	A	_____ (Miki / win) her match last week?
	B	No, she lost.
3	A	Where's Elena?
	B	She left ten minutes ago. She _____ (not / feel) very well.
4	A	When _____ (you / leave) school?
	B	In 1998.
5	A	_____ (you / buy) anything?
	B	No. It was all too expensive.
6	A	Why _____ (Sonia / go) home so early last night?
	B	She was really tired.
7	A	What was the film like?
	B	I _____ (not / enjoy) it.
8	A	_____ (your parents / pay) for the trip?
	B	No, I saved the money myself.

glossary

takeaway /ˈteɪkəweɪ/ (n) a meal from a restaurant that you eat at home

write it!

Write an article about your oldest school friend.

When did you meet?	Why did you get on?
How did you meet?	Do you still see each other now?

natural English *both*

9 Read the article in exercise 7 (on *p.7*) again. Are sentences 1 to 5 true ✓ or false ✗?

They both started school on the same day. ✓

1 Kate and Amanda both worked in the same shop at the weekend.
2 They both went to university in London.
3 They are both very tidy people.
4 They both love loud music.
5 Both of them moved out of the flat.

10 Simon and Marcus are twin brothers. Write sentences about them using *both*.

	Simon	**Marcus**
What sport do you like?	*football*	*football*
1 What do you study?	*engineering*	*engineering*
2 What are you good at?	*art*	*art*
3 Do you play an instrument?	*the guitar*	*the guitar*
4 What do you hate?	*waiting for things*	*waiting for things*
5 Where do you live?	*in Zurich*	*in Zurich*

They both like football. OR *Both of them like football.*

1 _____
2 _____
3 _____
4 _____
5 _____

 say it!

Say five things that are the same about you and your best friend or someone in your family.

> Sayuri and I both like singing.

 **expand** your grammar

neither

Notice that a singular verb is used after *neither* in written English.

Neither Karin **nor** Sabine <u>was</u> at the party. / **Neither of them** <u>was</u> at the party.
(= Karin wasn't at the party. Sabine wasn't at the party.)

Neither my brother **nor** I <u>speaks</u> French. / **Neither of us** <u>speaks</u> French.
(= My brother doesn't speak French. I don't speak French.)

Write sentences about Simon and Marcus using *neither*.

	Simon	Marcus
Do you have a job?	*Not at moment.*	*No.*
1 Do you smoke?	*No.*	*No I don't.*
2 Can you speak another language?	*No.*	*No.*
3 Do you live at home?	*No – by myself*	*No – with friends.*
4 Do you have a car?	*No – a motorbike.*	*No.*
5 Are you interested in computers?	*No.*	*Not at all.*

Neither Simon nor Marcus has a job at the moment. OR *Neither of them has a job at the moment.*

1 _____
2 _____
3 _____
4 _____
5 _____

Tick (✓) when you've done these sections.

natural English
☐ *have* + noun
☐ *a lot of, much, many, any*
☐ saying sorry

grammar
☐ countable / uncountable nouns
☐ adjectives and adverbs
☐ expand your grammar making uncountable nouns countable

vocabulary
☐ food
☐ restaurant language
☐ extreme adjectives
☐ expand your vocabulary gradable and extreme adjectives

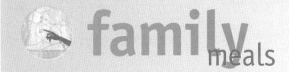

family meals

natural English *have* + noun

1 Order the words to make sentences. The first word is underlined.

    A you / lunch / have / <u>Did</u> ?
       Did you have lunch?
    B Yes, I had a sandwich at work.

1 **A** I'm going to the cafeteria. Do you want anything?
    B Yes please!   morning / didn't / this / breakfast / I / any / have .

2 **A** chocolate / day / have / every / <u>I</u> / some .

    B Me too!

3 **A** lunch / with / you / me / want / <u>Do</u> / have / to?

    B Sure. What time?

4 **A** What did you do for your mum's birthday?
    B had / a / restaurant / <u>We</u> / in / dinner / great .

5 **A** Coffee?
    B No thanks!   <u>I</u> / cups / had / three / morning / have / this .

6 **A** Do you want to go for a pizza?
    B I'm not hungry.   at / lunch / had / three / o'clock / <u>I</u> .

7 **A** Do you want to go to the cinema tonight?
    B I can't.   my / <u>I</u> / grandparents / dinner / am / with / having .

8 **A** Do you want something to eat?
    B have / a / I / biscuit / <u>Can</u> ?

 say it!

Answer the questions. Use *have* + noun.

Do you always have breakfast?
What do you usually have for lunch?
How often do you eat fast food?

Do you eat a lot of sweet things?
Do you drink a lot of tea or coffee?

I usually have cereal and some toast.

vocabulary food

2 Do the crossword. The pictures are your clues.

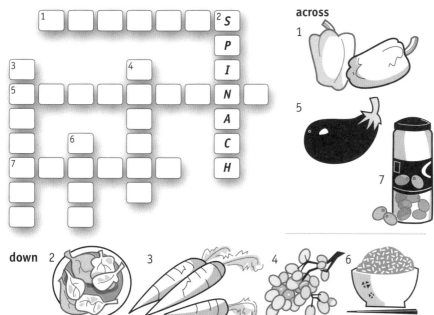

across
1
5
7

down 2 3 4 6

grammar countable/uncountable nouns

3 Natsuko is talking to Jane, her landlady in England. Put Natsuko's sentences, a to f, into the conversation.

Natsuko	_c_
Jane	No, it's nearly ready.
Natsuko	1_____
Jane	<u>Spaghetti</u> carbonara. It's pasta with bacon, cream, eggs, and cheese.
Natsuko	2_____
Jane	What's a typical evening meal in Japan?
Natsuko	3_____
Jane	OK, it's ready. Help yourself to bread. Do you eat much bread in Japan?
Natsuko	4_____
Jane	Well, that's healthy.
Natsuko	5_____
Jane	Sure, or there's juice in the fridge.

a Not much bread, no, but we eat a lot of rice.

b Sounds nice.

c ~~Do you need help with dinner?~~

d Can I get some water?

e What are you making?

f We eat a lot of noodles with vegetables, and fish. Actually, I don't eat much fish but most people do.

4 Underline nine more food and drink words in Jane and Natsuko's conversation which are uncountable.

natural English *a lot of, much, many, any*

5 Underline the correct word or words. (Sometimes two are possible.)

We haven't got <u>much</u> / many / <u>any</u> juice.

1 People from my country eat much / many / a lot of meat.

2 Are much / many / any of your friends coming to the party?

3 Have you got much / many / any homework tonight?

4 Do you do much / many / any exercise?

5 We play much / many / a lot of games in class.

6 I didn't have much / many / any lunch.

7 How much / many / a lot of people applied for the job?

8 I've got much / many / a lot of work to do today.

say it!

pronunciation Notice the stressed words in these sentences. Practise saying them.

| I <u>eat</u> a lot of <u>meat</u>. | I <u>don't</u> eat many <u>sweet</u> things. |
| I don't eat any <u>fish</u>. | I <u>don't</u> eat much <u>bread</u>. |

Now talk about what you eat and drink. Use these words.

| fast food | coffee | fish | pasta |
| meat | bread | sweet things | fizzy drinks |

expand your grammar

making uncountable nouns countable

coffee (U)
a coffee (C)
= a cup of coffee

orange juice (U)
an orange juice (C)
= a bottle or glass of orange juice

beer (U)
a beer (C)
= a can, a bottle, or a glass of beer

Look at some examples.

Can you get me **an** apple juice?

Could I have **two** coffees, please?

Who wants **a** beer?

I'd like **an** orange juice, please.

Notice the difference.

Do you like coffee?
= in general

Would you like a coffee?
= Do you want a cup of coffee now?

Match the sentences with the responses.

e	Do you want another beer?
1 ☐	I'd like two mineral waters, please.
2 ☐	Can you get me an orange juice?
3 ☐	Do you want a coffee?
4 ☐	There's no juice left.
5 ☐	I should drink more water.

a   Me too. I haven't had any today.

b   Do you want it in a glass or a bottle?

c   Yes please. Black, no sugar.

d   Fizzy or still?

e   ~~No thanks, but I'll have a cola.~~

f   That's OK, I'll get some later.

wordbooster

restaurant language

6   Match the beginnings and endings of these sentences.

	I'll have the prawns	a	for dessert.
1	Are you ready to	b	list.
2	I'd like the chicken for my main	c	all right?
3	Here's the wine	d	for my starter.
4	Enjoy your	e	menu now?
5	Is everything	f	meal.
6	Would you like to see the dessert	g	the bill, please?
7	I'd like chocolate cake	h	course.
8	Could I have	i	order?

extreme adjectives

7   Complete the sentences using words from the box.

terrible   ~~disgusting~~   brilliant   delicious   gorgeous   fabulous

This tastes absolutely _disgusting_ . I can't eat it.

1   Ben's new girlfriend is absolutely _____ . She could be a model.

2   The food was absolutely _____ . In fact it was probably the best meal I've ever had.

3   That's a _____ idea. You're so clever!

4   It was a _____ film – the worst I've seen all year.

5   **A** How was your holiday?
    B Fantastic. The hotel was _____ and we had a great time.

say it!

Talk about these things. Use your voice to show how you feel.

your last meal out   the last book you read
the last film you saw   your last holiday

It was absolutely disgusting!

expand your vocabulary

gradable and extreme adjectives

gradable	extreme
very, really, incredibly …	*absolutely, really …*
good	wonderful / fantastic
bad	terrible / dreadful
pretty	gorgeous
small	tiny
big	huge / enormous
hot	boiling
cold	freezing
interesting	fascinating
hungry	starving
tired	exhausted

Look at these examples.
A It's really **hot**, isn't it?
B Yes, it's absolutely **boiling**.
A Are you **tired**?
B I'm really **exhausted**.

Complete the sentences using the adjectives above.

A Was the party good?
B Absolutely *fantastic* ! We had a great time.

1 **A** Are you _____ ?
   B Absolutely starving! Let's have lunch.

2 **A** It's very _____ in here.
   B Yeah, I'm boiling. Will you open the windows?

3 **A** Their baby is incredibly small, isn't she?
   B Yes, she's really _____ .

4 **A** I'm going home. I'm really tired.
   B Me too. I'm absolutely _____ .

5 **A** Have you read this book? It's very _____ .
   B Yes. It's fascinating, isn't it?

6 **A** Do you think she's _____ ?
   B Yes, absolutely gorgeous.

7 **A** Is the water cold?
   B It's really _____ .

8 **A** Their apartment's quite big, isn't it?
   B It's _____ !

 # how to … be the perfect guest

natural English saying sorry

think back!

You're late for work. Think of four possible reasons.

8 Write sentences saying you're sorry and explaining why. Use the words given.

You're having a business meeting. You're late.
I'm sorry I'm late. My car broke down. (car / break down)
You invited a friend to your house for dinner. You've ordered a takeaway meal.
I didn't have time to cook anything. I'm really sorry. (no time / cook)

1 You're meeting a friend. You're late.
_____ . (miss / bus)

2 You're having dinner at a friend's house. You're late.
_____ . (get / lost)

3 You're having dinner at a friend's house. You haven't taken any wine.
_____ (no time / buy / wine)

4 You're meeting a friend for lunch. You're late.
_____ . (have / meeting / work)

5 It's your friend's birthday. You don't have a present for her.
_____ . (no time / buy / present)

say it!

pronunciation Notice the stressed words in these sentences. Practise saying them.

I'm <u>sorry</u> I'm <u>late</u>. My <u>car</u> broke down.
I didn't have <u>time</u> to <u>cook</u> anything. I'm <u>really</u> <u>sorry</u>.

That's OK …

You are the friend. Respond to the apologies in sentences 1 to 5.

grammar adjectives and adverbs

9 Complete the sentences using the word given as an adjective or an adverb.

Can you speak more _slowly_ please?   slow

She's very _quiet_ .   quiet

1 Those people were incredibly _____ .   kind

2 She plays the guitar really _____ .   good

3 You passed the test _____ .   easy

4 Don't get _____ . It was an accident.   angry

5 She always drives very _____ .   careful

6 It was a _____ match.   brilliant

7 The film was _____ dreadful.   absolute

8 Danish is _____ difficult to learn.   incredible

9 You look _____ . Is something wrong?   unhappy

10 Ask her _____ and she might help you.   nice

careful
absolute
easy **brilliant** QUIET
nice unhappy
good
angry *incredible*
slow *kind*

10 There are five more mistakes with adjectives and adverbs in the second e-mail. Correct them.

I'm having lunch with a colleague who's visiting us from Sweden. Where should I take her? Have you been to Bluewater Café?

terrible
Don't go to Bluewater Café! I had a ~~terribly~~ dinner there last week! We waited for our food for a long time. When it finally came my meal was cold and my friend's meal was disgusting! The waiter was incredible rude and when we complained the manager shouted at us. And the meal was expensive!

Why don't you go to Ceruttis? I had lunch there last Saturday and it was really well. The waitress served us very quick. The food was absolute delicious and it was quite cheaply. In fact, I'm thinking of going there again next Saturday for my girlfriend's birthday.

 write it!

Write your own response to the e-mail. Write about two restaurants or cafés in your area.

three

Tick (✓) when you've done these sections.

natural English
- [ ] *the best / worst thing about …*
- [ ] *once, twice,* etc.
- [ ] *a five-minute walk*
- [ ] asking where things are

grammar
- [ ] present perfect and past simple
- [ ] expand your grammar
  present perfect with *just*

vocabulary
- [ ] describing towns
- [ ] distance and time
- [ ] prepositional phrases
- [ ] expand your vocabulary
  places of interest

a strange place to live

natural English *the best / worst thing about …*

1 **Complete the sentences with phrases a to f.**

_____*c*_____ is that my apartment is always tidy! When I shared with other people the house was always a mess.

1 _____ is the people. We all get on really well, so it's fun being in the office.

2 _____ is that my parents still say that I have to be home by 11p.m. – even though I'm 21 now!

3 _____ is the money I spend on taxis as I hate waiting for the bus!

4 _____ is that everyone knows everything about each other. No one can have any secrets.

5 _____ is meeting people. It's hard work and sometimes difficult, but I love talking to people and helping them.

a The best thing about being a nurse
b The best thing about working here
c ~~The best thing about living alone~~
d The worst thing about not having my own car
e The worst thing about living at home
f The worst thing about living in a small town

say it!

What's the best and worst thing about …

your job or your school?   where you live?

grammar present perfect and past simple

2 Underline the correct verb forms.

A <u>Have you been</u> / Did you go to America?

B Yes. [1] I've been / I went there on holiday when [2] I've been / I was ten.

A Can you remember much about it?

B No, not really.

A Do you know Café Zibar?

B [3] I've heard / I heard of it, but [4] I've never been / I never went there. Why?

A [5] I've had / I had dinner there last night.

B [6] Has it been / Was it good?

A Yes, great!

A Gustavo's girlfriend is nice. [7] Have you met / Did you meet her?

B Yes, [8] we've met / we met at Danni's party last Saturday.

A Oh yeah. How was the party?

B Good. Why [9] haven't you gone / didn't you go?

A [10] I've finished / I finished work late.

3 Complete the sentences using the verb in either the past simple or present perfect.

<u>Have you studied</u> (you / study) any other languages?

1 I _____ (never meet) anyone from Vietnam before.

2 We _____ (finish) our exams three weeks ago.

3 They _____ (get) married in 1996.

4 _____ (you / see) the new James Bond movie?

5 _____ (you / go out) last night?

6 My dad _____ (buy) his first car in 1969!

7 My sister _____ (be) to England three times.

8 I _____ (live) in Germany all my life.

natural English *once, twice,* etc.

4 Look at the pictures and complete the questions. Do the quiz. Put a (✓) in the box to say how many times you've done something.

Your life – is it exciting, normal, or a bit quiet?

Have you ever...

	never	once	twice / a couple of times	a few times / 3 or 4 times	many times
... (be / on / plane)? *been on a plane?*					
... (do / dangerous sport)? _____					
... (meet / famous person)? _____					
... (sleep / outside)? _____					
... (be / surfing)? _____					
... (climb / mountain)? _____					
add up your points	**1**	**2**	**3**	**4**	**5**

Your life so far ...

20–30 Very exciting.

10–20 Quite normal – fun but safe.

0–10 A bit too quiet and calm. Try something new this week!

 say it!

Answer the quiz questions for yourself.

> I've been on a plane a couple of times. I've met lots of famous people.

 expand **your grammar**

present perfect with *just*

Look at these examples.

Tom's just arrived. OR
He arrived a few minutes ago.

Tom arrived.	now
✕		
7.28 p.m.	7.30 p.m.

I've just eaten. OR I ate ten minutes ago.

I ate.	now
✕		
1.50 p.m.	2.00 p.m.

They've just moved house. OR
They moved house last week.

They moved.	now
✕		
2nd March	9th March

**Write sentences with the same meaning.
Use the present perfect with *just*.**

   A   Can you give this to Jack?
   B   No. He left a minute or two ago.
       No. He *'s just left.*

1 A   That's a nice jacket.
   B   I bought it an hour ago.
       I _____

2 A   Hyo Sang's not here today.
   B   Yes he is. I saw him a few minutes ago.
       Yes he is. I _____

3 A   Have you read this book?
   B   Yes. I finished it earlier today.
       Yes. I _____

4 A   What's wrong with Sarah?
   B   She had an accident about
       ten minutes ago.
       She _____

5 A   What time's the next bus?
   B   You'll have to wait. One left about
       one minute ago.
       You'll have to wait. One

       _____

 wordbooster

describing towns

think back!

Think of …
– a country that is dangerous to visit at the moment.
– a place that you think is peaceful / attractive / lively.
– a building you know that is ugly.
– a place you sometimes go to that is noisy / polluted.

5 Complete the sentences using the words in the box.

> ugly   dangerous   peaceful   polluted   ~~noisy~~   lively   safe   quiet   clean

There was a disco under the hotel. It was really *noisy* _____ at night and I couldn't sleep.

1 The apartment is in a very _____ grey building. It's horrible.

2 You can't swim in the river any more because it's so _____ .

3 The food in my local restaurant is fantastic, but it's always _____ in there. I never have to book a table.

4 I don't feel _____ if I walk through the park in the evening. I prefer to stay on the main road.

5 That's a _____ part of the city. Don't go there alone.

6 The streets there are always very _____ . You never see any rubbish.

7 It's a _____ part of the city, especially in the evening as there are lots of clubs and bars there.

8 We stayed in a holiday house outside the city. It was a really _____ place right on the beach with no one else around.

distance and time

6 Order the words to make sentences.

> school / It / near / 's / the .
> _It's near the school_ .

1 from / the / far / It / station / 's / not / train .

_____

2 near / 's / hospital / quite / It / the .

_____

3 a / from / centre / way / It / city / long / the / 's .

_____

4 from / Is / far / here / it ?

_____

5 way / house / long / from / my / It / quite / a / 's .

_____

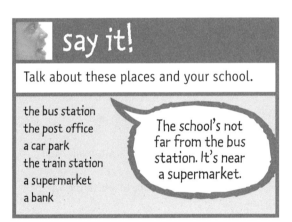

say it!

Talk about these places and your school.

the bus station
the post office
a car park
the train station
a supermarket
a bank

> The school's not far from the bus station. It's near a supermarket.

natural English _a five-minute walk_

7 Complete the sentences using the words given.

> I don't drive to work. It's only _a ten-minute walk_ . (a walk / 10 minutes)

1 You could get the train. It's _____ (a journey / 50 minutes) from here.

2 It's _____ (a flight / 20 hours) from England to Australia.

3 It's _____ (a drive / 1 hour) to my grandparents' house.

4 I'm doing _____ (a course / 12 weeks).

5 She's going on _____ (a tour / 2 weeks) of Europe.

how to ...
get around town

vocabulary prepositional phrases

8 Kelly is looking for somewhere to live. She has information about five flats in different parts of her city. Complete the sentences using the words from the box.

road	near	right	close	just	corner
~~next~~	opposite	end	round	edge	

A

The flat is _____next_____ to a hotel
¹_____ in the centre of town. It's
lively at night, which is fun, but it can be a
bit noisy and it's sometimes dangerous.

B

It's in a really quiet area on the ²_____ of town. It's no good
if you want nightclubs or shops nearby, but it's peaceful. There's a
bus stop ³_____ outside the flat and buses to the city every
20 minutes.

C

It's quite ⁴_____ the centre. It's on the ⁵_____ of two
busy streets and it's an ugly building, but inside the flat's very nice.
There's a cinema down the ⁶_____ .

D

It's a really small flat but it's very ⁷_____ to the centre.
It's not far from the train station and there's a supermarket
⁸_____ the corner.

E

It's ⁹_____ a park so your bedroom
looks over the trees. It's a very safe part of
town and there's a shopping centre at the
¹⁰_____ of the road. It's expensive
though.

write it!

A friend is coming to live in your flat for two weeks while you are
on holiday. Write an e-mail describing where you live.

natural English asking where things are

9 You want to find these places. Write questions using the words given.

car park (near)?

A *Is there a car park near here?*

B There's one just down the road.

1 bank (nearest)?

A _____

B There's one opposite the supermarket.

2 post office (far)?

A _____

B It's a twenty-minute-walk.

3 supermarket (near)?

A _____

B It's just round the corner.

4 train station (far)?

A _____

B It's about ten minutes by bus.

5 bus stop (nearest)?

A _____

B There's one next to the school.

 say it!

pronunciation
Underline the stressed words in the questions in exercise 9. Practise asking and answering them.

> Is there a
> car park near
> here?

You are outside your school. Imagine someone asks you these questions. Answer them.

---

 expand your vocabulary

places of interest

Match the places and activities.

an information centre	a look at paintings
1 an art gallery	b buy things (inside)
2 a stadium /ˈsteɪdiəm/	c buy things (outside)
3 a museum /mjuˈziːəm/	d watch or play sport
4 a theatre /ˈθɪətə/	e watch a play or a concert
5 an open-air market	f look at things from the past
6 a shopping centre	g find out about a city and get maps
7 a fun park	h look at fish and other sea creatures
8 an aquarium /əˈkweəriəm/	i go on fairground rides and play games

Complete the sentences from a guidebook to Vancouver. Use the words from the box.

Playland Fun Park	B.C. Place Stadium	Vancouver Museum
Vancouver Art Gallery	open-air market	~~Vancouver Little Theatre~~
information centre	Vancouver Aquarium	shopping centres

- *Vancouver Little Theatre* has productions by national and international companies.
- 1 _____ exhibits the paintings of Canadian and international artists.
- Vancouver has 2 _____ everywhere! Go to Granville Mall for department stores and Robson Street for clothing.
- 3 _____ seats 60,000 people. It's home to one of the top Canadian Football league teams.
- You can learn about Canadian history and culture at the 4 _____
- 5 _____ is in the east of Stanley Park. Among more than 8,000 aquatic animals on display are whales, sea lions, sharks, and crocodiles.
- Get maps of the city from the 6 _____ on Hornsby Street.
- 7 _____ features lots of amusements, including a merry-go-round, a rollercoaster, a games arcade, and a small zoo.
- Every Sunday on Granville Island there's a huge 8 _____ where you can buy arts, crafts, clothes, and fresh produce.

test yourself!

Look at the places (1 to 8) again. Do you have any of these places in your hometown?

Now cover the words on the left and remember the places.
You find out about a city in an information centre.

four   buy it

shop till you drop

natural English *this/that (one), these/those (ones)*

1 Match the questions and responses.

c	Can you pass me my jacket?
1	Which bag do you think I should take?
2	Are you going to wear your black trousers?
3	Shall we take this table?
4	Is that my book?
5	Do you think she'd like the yellow flowers?

a No. This one's mine.

b No, get her those ones by the counter. She loves red.

c ~~Is this one yours?~~

d Take that one. It's really big.

e No, I'm wearing these.

f No, let's sit at that one, over by the window.

 say it!

Cover the responses a to f. Look at the pictures and respond to questions 1 to 5.

Is this one yours?

unit four   **19**

natural English *can/can't afford*

2 Write sentences with the same meaning. Use *can't afford to (do sth)*.

My phone bill is really big. I can't pay it.
I can't afford to pay my phone bill.

1   He's saving to buy a car but he needs a lot more money.

_____

2   I'd like to go to the concert but it's too expensive for me.

_____

3   I need new shoes but I can't buy them at the moment.

_____

4   We'd love to stay in a hotel but we don't have the money.

_____

5   I want to take a taxi but I haven't got enough money.

_____

grammar *will* for spontaneous decisions and offers

3 Complete the text messages using *will* and the verbs in the box.

send	bring	meet	call	give	~~book~~

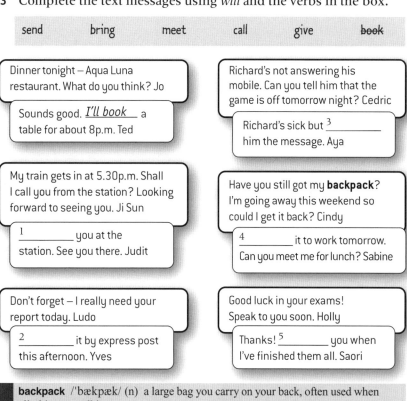

Dinner tonight – Aqua Luna restaurant. What do you think? Jo

Sounds good. *I'll book* ___ a table for about 8p.m. Ted

Richard's not answering his mobile. Can you tell him that the game is off tomorrow night? Cedric

Richard's sick but ³_____ him the message. Aya

My train gets in at 5.30p.m. Shall I call you from the station? Looking forward to seeing you. Ji Sun

¹_____ you at the station. See you there. Judit

Have you still got my **backpack**? I'm going away this weekend so could I get it back? Cindy

⁴_____ it to work tomorrow. Can you meet me for lunch? Sabine

Don't forget – I really need your report today. Ludo

²_____ it by express post this afternoon. Yves

Good luck in your exams! Speak to you soon. Holly

Thanks! ⁵_____ you when I've finished them all. Saori

backpack /'bækpæk/ (n) a large bag you carry on your back, often used when climbing or walking

write it!

Write responses to these two text messages. Make an offer using *will*.

✉ I'm arriving on 22nd May and I need somewhere to stay for three nights. Can you help? Carola

✉ The party's at 7p.m. Please bring some food or drink. See you there. Tony

---

expand *your grammar*

will for requests and *shall* for offers

We can use *will* for a request (when we are asking someone else to do something).
<u>Will</u> you help me carry these bags?
<u>Will</u> you give Sonia a message?

We can use *shall* for an offer (when <u>we</u> are offering to do something for another person).
<u>Shall</u> I call a taxi for you?
<u>Shall</u> I open the window?

Underline the correct word.

Will / <u>Shall</u> I answer the phone?

1   Do you feel sick? Will / Shall I get you some water?

2   I'm too busy to go out for lunch. Will / Shall you get me a sandwich?

3   Will / Shall I make us a coffee?

4   Are you going to the post office? Will / Shall you post this?

5   Will / Shall you help me with my homework?

say it!

Make these requests to a colleague.

help me with this report
e-mail me that report tomorrow
give me that book
help me with something

Will you help me with this report?

Make these offers to a friend.

make us some dinner
get you a coffee
call you later
drive tonight

Shall I make us some dinner?

wordbooster

clothes

think back!

Remember the words for all the clothes you are wearing now.

4 Meg and Owen are packing their suitcases for a holiday. Write the words for the clothes in the pictures.

Owen What are you taking?

Meg I'm definitely taking these _____ and (1) _____ .

Owen Are you taking anything smart?

Meg (2) _____ and (3) _____ .

Owen Do you think I need to take (4) _____ ?

Meg No, you can wear (5) _____ and (6) _____ – that looks smart.

Owen So I don't need to take (7) _____ ?

Meg No.

Owen Are you taking all those shoes?

Meg No, just my sandals and a pair of (8) _____ . I'm going to wear (9) _____ on the plane.

Owen Are you taking (10) _____ ?

Meg Yes, it might be cold in the evening.

trousers _____

1 _____   6 _____

2 _____   7 _____

3 _____   8 _____

4 _____   9 _____

5 _____   10 _____

test yourself!

Read the conversation saying the words for the clothes in the pictures.

5 Write W if you wear this or C if you carry it.

trainers *W*

1 a handbag ___   5 glasses ___

2 an umbrella ___   6 a bracelet ___

3 a belt ___   7 a briefcase ___

4 make-up ___   8 a necklace ___

say it!

pronunciation Underline the stressed syllables and practise saying the words.

Complete the questions with *wear* or *carry*. Then answer them.

Do you usually _____ a briefcase, a handbag, or a backpack?

Do you often _____ jewellery? What kind?

Do you have to _____ glasses or contact lenses?

phrasal verbs (1)

6 Complete the sentences using the verbs given. You will need to add a pronoun (e.g. *it*) and an adverb or preposition (e.g. *on*).

A I can't get the fan to work.

B Press the green button to *turn it on* _____ . (turn)

1 **A** I like these jeans.

B Why don't you _____ ? (try)

2 **A** You've dropped your keys.

B Can you _____ ? (pick)

3 **A** This new DVD player doesn't work.

B You should _____ . (take)

4 **A** Do you still want the TV on?

B No, _____ . (turn)

5 **A** I can't find my wallet.

B Did you _____ somewhere in the kitchen? (put)

how to buy clothes

vocabulary shopping

7 Complete the sentences using the words in the box.

> fit   size   on   counter   changing   bigger

I tried _on_ ten shirts but none of them looked right.

1 There was one pair of shoes I liked but they didn't have my _____.

2 We haven't got it in a _____ size but our other shop in the city might have one.

3 I think I left my wallet on the _____ when I was paying.

4 The _____ rooms are full at the moment. Can you wait?

5 This jacket's almost new but it doesn't _____ me any more. Do you want it?

natural English talking about size

8 Find eight more mistakes in the conversation between the customer and the shop assistant. Correct them.

       try them on

c Can I try on them, please?

sa What size are you?

c 39, I think.

sa We haven't got any in 39 but you can try 38½ .

c OK … No, they doesn't fit. They is a bit small.

sa How's the shirt?

c It's a wrong size. It be too tight.

sa What are you size?

c I'm usually ten.

sa OK, if the ten's too small I'll look for a twelve.

sa How's that one?

c Much better.

sa It look good on you. It's a great colour.

c It's nice, isn't it? Where pay?

grammar *too* and *very*, *too much / many*

9 Complete the sentences using *be + too* and a word from the box.

> dangerous   young   tired   expensive   far   dark   late   difficult   cold

I don't want you to buy a motorbike. They *'re too dangerous* .

1 I can't afford to buy a new car at the moment. The one I want _____ .

2 It _____ to drive there. It would take at least ten hours.

3 **A** Hurry up.
  B We _____. The bus has gone.

4 This class _____ for me. I think I should change class.

5 **A** Are you coming to the cinema with us?
  B No. I _____. I'm going home to bed!

6 **A** Do you want to go to the beach?
  B Not really! It _____ to swim today.

7 It _____ in here. Will you turn the light on?

8 **A** Do you think Monika should get the job?
  B No, she _____. She's only 19!

10 Underline the correct word.

Hi Jessica,

How are you? Is it cold at home at the moment? It's *very / too* hot here so I go to the beach nearly every day after school!

I'm really enjoying myself. Classes are ¹ *very / too* different from our old school. We speak a lot and the teachers are ² *very / too* young. The first class was ³ *very / too* difficult for me so I changed to a different level. The teacher's good; the lessons are ⁴ *very / too* lively and I'm learning a lot.

I live in a big house with some other students. It's ⁵ *very / too* far to walk to school but it only takes 15 minutes on the bus. I share a room with another girl.

Next week a group of us are going camping for the weekend. I think it'll be fun.

See you,

Ellen

Jessica

24 Elm

Oxford

OX2 6B

© F. Peddick ✐ 00 3278 22 94

11 Write new sentences with the same meanings. Use *too many / much* and the words given.

The roads are too busy.
There's _too much traffic_ . (traffic)

1 This tea's too sweet.
It's got _____ in it. (sugar)

2 Your essay is too long.
You've written _____. (words)

3 It's too expensive.
It costs _____. (money)

4 The class is too big.
There are _____ in the class. (students)

5 The beach was really crowded.
There were _____ on the beach. (people)

say it!

Say the sentences using *too much / many* and a suitable noun.

We've ordered _____.

Are you coming for a drink?

No. I've got _____ to do.

That bag's got _____ in it.

expand your vocabulary

commonly confused words

Notice how these words are used.

price (n) What's the price?

cost (vb) How much does it cost?
It costs $500.

pay (vb) Can I pay <u>by</u> credit card?
My boss paid <u>for</u> our lunch.
She paid $70 <u>for</u> it.
I'll pay <u>for</u> you if you haven't got enough money.

buy (vb) Where did you buy it?
Can I buy you a coffee?

Make new sentences with the same meanings. Use *price*, *cost*, *buy*, *pay*, and any other necessary words.

She left her wallet at work, so I paid for her coffee.
She left her wallet at work, so I _bought her_ a coffee.

1 I'd like to use my chequebook.
Can I _____ cheque?

2 The tickets were $25 each.
The tickets _____ each.

3 Did you pay for the tickets?
Did you _____ the tickets?

4 How much does it cost?
What's the _____?

5 That jacket cost him $100.
He _____ for that jacket.

6 Would you like a drink?
Can I _____ a drink?

7 Thanks for helping me! Let me buy you lunch.
Thanks for helping me! Let me _____ your lunch.

8 What did you pay for it?
How much did it _____?

Tick (✓) when you've done these sections.

natural English
- ☐ *How do you spell ... ?*
- ☐ asking for permission
- ☐ *what / when you like*
- ☐ saying if things are true
- ☐ giving instructions / advice

grammar
- ☐ *can / can't, have to / don't have to*
- ☐ *had to / didn't have to / did you have to ...?*
- ☐ expand your grammar *have got to*

vocabulary
- ☐ study centre
- ☐ verb + noun collocation
- ☐ expand your vocabulary school subjects

 how to ...
use a study centre

natural English *How do you spell ...?*

1   Ana is on the phone to a language school. Order the lines of the conversation.

receptionist	_b_		**receptionist**
Ana	1	a	OK. And your first name?
receptionist	2	b	~~First of all, what's your surname?~~
Ana	3	c	Do you spell it with double n?
receptionist	4	d	Right. What's your address?
Ana	5	e	Strohmeier. How do you spell it?
receptionist	6		**Ana**
Ana	7	f	S-T-R-O-H-M-E-I-E-R
receptionist	8	g	No, just one.
		h	Ana.
		i	Strohmeier.

say it!

Imagine you are giving this information over the phone. Spell your ...

| family name. | the name of your street. | the name of your town or city. |

vocabulary study centre

2 Find the words for these things in the puzzle.

CD _____

1 _____

2 _____

3 _____

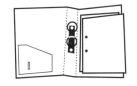

4 _____

5 _____

6 cassette ...

7 _____

8 _____

C	C	B	O	O	T	T	P	F	H	A
P	H	O	T	O	C	O	P	I	E	R
Y	U	O	M	I	V	I	R	L	A	E
B	O	K	J	P	F	I	L	E	D	C
C	A	S	S	E	U	C	D	K	P	O
H	B	H	E	A	D	T	N	E	H	P
W	P	E	C	O	M	P	E	R	O	H
F	I	L	T	D	T	F	G	R	N	O
M	H	F	R	E	C	O	R	D	E	R
C	A	S	S	E	T	T	E	L	S	E

grammar *can / can't, have to / don't have to*

3 Read the information about a language school. Underline the correct words.

You <u>have to</u> / don't have to be in class by 8.30 a.m.

1 You have to / don't have to take a test every week.

2 You can / can't speak your own language in class.

3 You have to / don't have to buy a coursebook from the bookshop.

4 You have to / don't have to take your own paper or notebook to class.

5 You have to / don't have to do homework every day.

6 You can / can't use the computer room at lunchtime.

7 You have to / don't have to have 100% attendance to get a certificate.

8 You can / can't drink in the classrooms.

TESTING All students take a test once every 4 weeks.

ENGLISH ONLY Please speak only English in class. It's the best way to improve your English quickly and make friends from all over the world.

MATERIALS Your teacher will give you a coursebook on the first day of class. You will need to bring a notebook or paper to class.

HOMEWORK Homework is an important part of your programme. Your teacher will set homework every day.

COMPUTERS The computer room is open every afternoon from 3.00 – 5.00 p.m.

CERTIFICATES You will receive a certificate when you finish your course (if your attendance has been above 90%).

REGULATIONS No food or drinks in the classrooms.

Timetable		
8.30 – 10.00 a.m.	10.00 – 10.30 a.m.	10.30 – 12.00 p.m.
class	coffee break	class

grammar *had to / didn't have to / did you have to ...?*

4 Complete the sentences. Use *have to* in the correct present or past form with the verbs given.

Hiroyuki _has to be_ (be) here at 6 if he wants to come with us.
I couldn't afford the airfare so I _had to sell_ (sell) my car to pay for the ticket.

1 When I was younger I _____ (be) home by 8 p.m.

2 What time _____ (you / start) work tomorrow?

3 We _____ (go) to school yesterday. It was a national holiday.

4 _____ (you / wear) a uniform when you were at school?

5 You _____ (buy) your ticket over the Internet to get that price.

6 I _____ (work) tomorrow, so shall we go out?

7 Robert's not coming tonight. He _____ (look / after) his little sister.

8 He _____ (come) if he doesn't want to.

9 We missed the bus so we _____ (get) a taxi home.

10 _____ (he / speak) English at work?

 **expand** your grammar

have got to

> **In spoken and informal written English we often use *have got to* instead of *have to*.**
>
> I've got to do some shopping later.
>
> He's got to help his brother.
>
> Have you got to work tomorrow?
>
> **It's not possible to use *have got to* in the past.**
>
> I had ~~got~~ to go. ✗   I had to go. ✔

Write sentences using the words given.

I / got / buy a birthday present.
I've got to buy a birthday present.

1 I / got / study tonight.

_____

2 you / got / work / this weekend?

_____

3 She / got / help her sister.

_____

4 You / got / be there at 8 p.m.

_____

5 We / got / leave now.

_____

natural English asking for permission

5 You are staying at someone's house. Ask for permission to do these things using the words given.

use the phone (OK)
Is it OK if I use the phone?   _f_

1 have a shower (can)

_____   _____

2 make a coffee (OK)

_____   _____

3 turn on the TV (can)

_____   _____

4 check my e-mails (OK)

_____   _____

5 use the washing machine (OK)

_____   _____

Match the requests with responses a to f.

a Yeah, no <u>problem</u>. The remote control's on the bookcase.

b Yes, of <u>course</u>. I'll get you a towel.

c No, I'm <u>sorry</u> you <u>can't</u>. I'm using the computer at the moment.

d No problem. I'll show you how it works.

e No, sorry, I don't have any.

f ~~Yes, of course. You can use the one in the study.~~

 say it!

Ask for permission to do these things.

borrow an umbrella	
close the window	Can I / Is it OK if
turn on the radio	I borrow an
use the microwave	umbrella?

pronunciation Notice the stressed words (underlined) in a to c. Now practise the responses.

wordbooster

think back!

Remember a place you go to study when you are three or four/eight/fourteen/twenty years old.   *nursery school*

verb + noun collocation

6 Complete the sentences. Use the verbs from the box in the correct form.

pass	take	revise	leave	~~make~~
join	miss	go	wear	

At first I found the course really difficult but now I *'m making* progress!

1 I've always wanted to be an actor. When I was 12 I _____ the drama club at school.

2 If I _____ my exams, I want to go to university.

3 We had to _____ an awful school uniform. I hated it.

4 I was really sick last month and I _____ a lot of lessons.

5 I _____ school last year to work for my dad.

6 I'm only 15. I have to _____ to school for one more year.

7 I can't work tonight. I've got to _____ for my exams.

8 If I fail, I'll work for a year then _____ my exams again next year.

write it!

You are writing an e-mail to a friend from another country. Write a paragraph about your education.

I started primary school when I was five. It was a small school and my mum was a teacher there ...

expand your vocabulary

school subjects

Match the words and pictures.

f languages /ˈlæŋgwɪdʒɪz/	
1 ☐ maths /ˈmæθs/	5 ☐ chemistry /ˈkemɪstri/
2 ☐ history /ˈhɪstri/	6 ☐ geography /dʒiˈɒgrəfi/
3 ☐ biology /baɪˈɒlədʒi/	7 ☐ art /ɑːt/
4 ☐ physical education (PE) /ˈfɪzɪkl ˌedʒuˈkeɪʃn/	8 ☐ economics /ˌiːkəˈnɒmɪks/

say it!

Cover the words, look at the pictures and test yourself. Now answer these questions.

What is/was your favourite subject at school?
What are/were you good at?
What are/were you bad at?
Which subjects have you taken exams in?

I liked history.

natural English *what / when you like*

7 Complete the sentences using *what* or *when I / you / we like.*

> We can use the Internet when we like.

A Do you ever surf the Internet at work?

B Yes. We can use the Internet
when we like _____ .

1 **A** Do you have to wear anything special?

  B No, I can wear _____ .
  I usually wear jeans and a T-shirt.

2 **A** What time do you have to start?

  B I work flexi time. That means I can
  start _____ but I have to
  work for seven hours each day.

3 **A** Do you have a fixed lunch break?

  B We can go to lunch _____
  but only for one hour.

4 **A** Can you take coffee breaks
  _____ ?

  B Yes, but not too often!

5 **A** Do you have to work hard?

  B Not really! I can do _____ .
  My boss never looks at my work!

taking exams

natural English saying if things are true

8 Order the words to make sentences.

> not / 'm / sure / that / true / I / 's   *I'm sure that's not true.*

1 true / think / 's / that / I   _____

2 right / 's / that   _____

3 that / think / I / 's / true / don't   _____

4 'm / sure / I / that / about / not   _____

5 depends / it   _____

---

say it!

pronunciation Underline the stressed words
in sentences 1 to 5. Practise saying the sentences.
Do you think these statements are true or not true?

> I'm sure that's not true.

1 More people speak English as a first language than any other
language in the world.

2 There are about 1,500 languages in the world.

3 All pilots on international flights speak in English on the radio.

4 English is the most difficult language to learn.

see answers at bottom of page

---

natural English giving instructions / advice

9 Takanori is going to study in America. He has asked an English-speaking friend for advice about learning English. Complete his friend's letter with words and phrases a to f.

> __c__ a newspaper or magazine every day, but ¹____ every word
> that you don't know. You should enjoy reading it! ²____ to speak
> English all the time. You'll meet other students from Japan but
> ³____ to them in Japanese. ⁴____ a Japanese-English dictionary.
> You don't always find the right word because English words often
> have lots of different meanings. Get an English-English dictionary
> and use both if you need to. ⁵____ watch some TV or listen to the
> radio. You might not understand everything but that doesn't matter.

a It's a good idea to   d Try

b don't talk   e don't look up

c ~~Read~~   f It's not a good idea to use

Tick (✓) when you've done these sections.

natural English

☐ *a bit (of)*
☐ *what sort / kind of...?*
☐ vague language: *around, about, or so*

grammar

☐ superlative adjectives
☐ comparative adjectives
☐ *will / be going to* for prediction
☐ expand your grammar
  the / (-) with places

vocabulary

☐ parts of a country
☐ weather conditions
☐ climate and temperature
☐ expand your vocabulary
  superlatives + *in / of*

 how to compare things

vocabulary parts of a country

1 Match the sentences with the places on the map of Australia. The places may be chosen more than once.

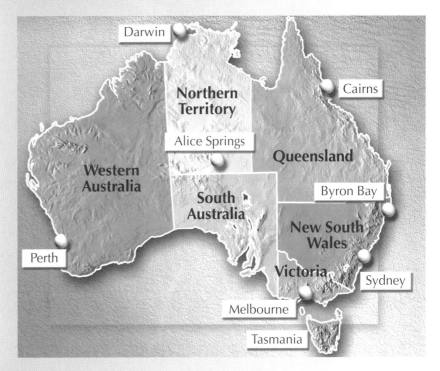

	It's on the south-east coast.	*Sydney*
1	It's on the east coast.	
2	It's on the north-east coast.	
3	It's on the west coast.	
4	It's in the south.	
5	It's in the centre.	
6	It's in the north.	
7	It's near the Queensland border.	
8	It's an island off the south coast.	

 say it!

Cover the sentences. Look at the map again and say where the places are.

> Sydney's on the south-east coast.

grammar superlative adjectives

2 Right ✓ or wrong ✗? If the grammar is wrong, correct it.

Australia

Australia is the world's ~~bigest~~ island.   ✗ *biggest*

1 It is the world's smallest continent.   _____

2 It contains the most large desert in the world outside the Sahara.   _____

3 It is home to oldest rainforest in the world.   _____

4 It has the longest coral reef in the world – over 2,000 km.   _____

5 It is the world's flattest and dryest land after Antarctica.   _____

6 Some of the tallest trees in the world are located on the south-west coast.   _____

7 It is home to the poisonousest snakes and spiders in the world.   _____

8 People say that Sydney has the good harbour in the world.   _____

3 Complete the sentences using the words given.

It was *the most difficult* test I've ever taken.   difficult

1 Peter's _____ person I know.   clever

2 Skydiving is _____ thing I've ever done.   exciting

3 It's _____ club in town.   popular

4 It was _____ holiday I've ever had.   bad

5 She's _____ girl I've ever met.   beautiful

6 I'm _____ child in my family.   young

7 It was _____ film I've seen this year.   good

8 It was _____ day of my life.   important

expand
your vocabulary

superlatives + *in* / *of*

Superlatives are often followed by a prepositional phrase with *in* or *of*.
Sydney is the largest city <u>in Australia</u>.
January is usually the hottest month <u>of the year</u>.

Complete the sentences using these phrases.

a in the world
b ~~in the street~~
c in my class
d in France
e in the shop
f of the week
g of the year
h of the day
i of my life

She lives in the biggest house <u>*in the street*</u> .

1 I think Canada is the biggest country _____ .

2 I often go for a walk at sunset – it's the best time _____ .

3 They were the most expensive shoes _____ .

4 Eun Kyung's the best student _____ .

5 Where I work Monday's always the busiest day _____ .

6 This is midsummer – the longest day _____ .

7 The Eiffel Tower is the most famous building _____ .

8 I'll never forget it. It was the best day _____ .

write it!

You are helping to write a guidebook about your country in English. Write some facts about places in your country. For example:

| the biggest city | the most popular sport |
| the hottest month | the best time of year to visit |

expand your grammar

the / (-) with places

Use *the* for these places.

oceans / seas / rivers / deserts
the Pacific, the Red Sea, the Thames,
the Sahara

groups of mountains / islands
the Alps, the Bahamas

certain countries
the United Kingdom, the Czech Republic,
the USA

Don't use *a* / *the* for these places.

continents / most countries / states
Europe, Argentina, California

lakes / most single mountains
Lake Victoria, Mount Fuji

towns / streets / squares
Budapest, Baker Street, Parliament Square

Cross out *the* if it is wrong.

I live on ~~the~~ Mackay Street.

1 Maria Carmen comes from the South America.

2 He lives near the Independence Square.

3 They're going to the Andes.

4 Have you been to the Cairo?

5 We stayed in a hotel on the Lake Louise.

6 I've been to the Mount Kilimanjaro.

7 We took a river cruise down the Amazon.

8 We went to Disneyland in the Florida.

9 I'd like to visit the Czech Republic.

10 My sister goes to the Canaries every year.

Try this quiz.

What's the world's ...

1 highest mountain? _____

2 longest river? _____

3 biggest desert? _____

4 smallest country? _____

5 largest ocean? _____

(The answers are at the bottom of the page.)

grammar comparative adjectives

4 Caroline is in Australia. She is talking to a travel agent about these two bus tours from Sydney to Cairns. Complete the sentences using comparative adjectives.

East Coast Experience
Sydney to Cairns
14 days

Maximum:
20 people

Accommodation:
Hostels and campsites

Price:
AUD $1,200

Travel North
Sydney to Cairns
12 days

MAXIMUM:
12 people

ACCOMMODATION:
Hotels

PRICE:
AUD $1,800

Caroline	What's the difference between them?
travel agent	The East Coast Experience is *longer* (long).
Caroline	But why is the Travel North trip [1] _____ (expensive)?
travel agent	It's a [2] _____ (small) group of people, the bus is [3] _____ (comfortable) and you stay in hotels.
Caroline	Which one do you think is [4] _____ (lively)?
travel agent	East Coast Experience is [5] _____ (relaxed) and [6] _____ (young) people usually choose that one. It's also [7] _____ (cheap).
Caroline	I think East Coast sounds [8] _____ (good).

say it!

Cover the exercise and compare the two trips using these adjectives.

The Travel North trip is shorter.

short   big   long   comfortable   expensive

wordbooster

weather conditions

think back!

Remember the words for the different types of weather shown in the pictures.

5 Complete the sentences with suitable words. Use the pictures above to help you.

I don't like driving in *fog* .
It's difficult to see where you're going.

1 I'm going skiing next month. I hope there's lots of _____ .

2 My boyfriend really likes going sailing on _____ days. It's a lot more fun!

3 Bring an umbrella. It's going to _____ later.

4 If it's _____ tomorrow we can go to the beach.

5 It's very _____ .
Do you think it's going to rain?

climate and temperature

6 Read the text and match the graphs with the places.

a Darwin – in the far north. _____

b Hobart – in the south. _____

c Alice Springs – in the centre. _____

■ Australian seasons are the opposite of those in Europe and North America. It's summer in December and winter in July and August. There are big differences in the climate in different parts of the country. The south has cold winters. Conditions can be icy and it sometimes snows, while summers are pleasant and warm. As you go north the climate gets hotter. In the far north there are just two seasons: hot and wet, and hot and dry. From October to December there are afternoon storms with thunder and showers, while very heavy rain falls through January and February. The centre of Australia is very dry and the temperature varies a lot. It can rise to above 40 degrees Celsius during the day in summer, and fall to below freezing on winter nights.

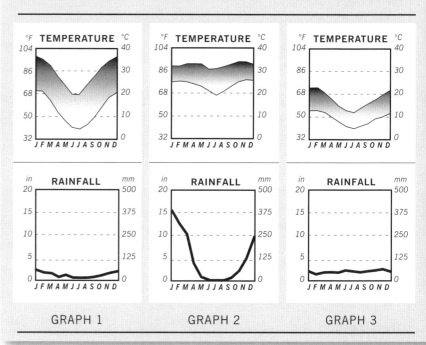

GRAPH 1   GRAPH 2   GRAPH 3

natural English *a bit (of)*

7 Add *of* to the sentences if necessary.

A We're going to miss the train.

B No, we've still got a bit *of* time.

1 A Shall we get some lunch?

B Yes, I'm a bit hungry.

2 A It's incredibly hot outside.

B It's a bit cooler in here.

3 A What was the weather like?

B We had a bit rain.

4 A What's Jake's girlfriend like?

B She's a bit unfriendly.

5 A I can't afford to get a taxi.

B I've got a bit money.

looking ahead

natural English *what sort / kind of ...?*

8 Complete the questions.

What sort of food —	a do you drive?
1 What kind of work	b do you like eating?
2 What sort of car	c do you listen to?
3 What kind of music	d do you enjoy watching?
4 What sort of place	e do you do?
5 What kind of films	f do you live in?

Match the questions with these answers.

a ☐ I share an apartment with a friend.

b ☐ Actually, I've got a motorbike.

c ☐ I'm a lawyer.

d ☐0☐ ~~I love anything spicy.~~

e ☐ Pop, jazz – anything really.

f ☐ I usually prefer comedies or thrillers.

Answer the questions about yourself.

grammar *will / be going to* for prediction

9 Complete the sentences. Use the words given and *will / won't* or *be going to* for prediction. Both forms are sometimes possible.

He *'s sure he won't get* the job. (sure / he / not get) OR
He *'s sure he isn't going to get* the job.

1 My mum _____ . (think / they / get married)

2 I _____ any problems. (sure / there / not / be)

3 Don't wait for Thiago. He _____ late. (probably / be)

4 I _____ . (not think / it / rain)

5 It's a good film. I _____ it. (sure / you / enjoy)

6 What time _____ home? (you / think / you / be)

7 They _____ me some money for my birthday. (probably / give)

8 Carrie _____ the exam. (not / think / she / pass)

9 It's late. I _____ a taxi home. (think / I / get)

10 I'll see you at the party. _____ there? (you / sure / you be)

natural English vague language: *around, about, or so*

10 Complete the sentences. Use the words given and the numbers and words from the box.

6 o'clock	$50	100km	a week	half an hour
1.8m	50 people	30 years	~~1,000 words~~	

The essay's got to be *around 1,000 words* long.   around

1 I think I'll be _____ . Will you wait for me?   or so

2 It'll take us an hour and a half to drive. It's _____ away.   about

3 Can we meet at _____ ?   around

4 She's been in hospital for _____ .   or so

5 My brother's _____ tall.   about

6 She's _____ old.   around

7 I think the tickets cost _____ .   about

8 There were _____ at the party.   around

Tick (✓) when you've done these sections.

natural English
- [ ] link words and phrases
- [ ] *have a good / bad time*
- [ ] uses of *get*
- [ ] asking how to say things

grammar
- [ ] past simple and past continuous
- [ ] expand your grammar
  past continuous with *while*

vocabulary
- [ ] phrases with *go*
- [ ] irregular verbs
- [ ] phrasal verbs (2)
- [ ] expand your vocabulary synonyms

how to tell a story

vocabulary phrases with *go*

1 Add the words *for*, *to*, or *and* if necessary.

Mum's gone *for* a walk.

1 Do you want to go see a film tonight?

2 She's gone the cinema.

3 I usually go a run in the mornings.

4 My family goes skiing together every winter.

5 Are you going Soraya's party on Friday?

6 I have to go buy a birthday present for my brother.

7 I'm going shopping this afternoon. Do you want to come?

8 Shall we go a meal before the film tonight?

say it!

pronunciation Practise saying sentences 1 to 8. Don't forget:

go and /ɡəʊən/   go for a /ɡəʊfərə/   go to a /ɡəʊtuːə/

Answer these questions using the words given.

> I'm going to a nightclub.

What are you doing this evening?	go / a nightclub.
What are you doing after class today?	go / swimming.
Have you got any plans for the weekend?	have to / go / see / friend.
Do you play any sport?	usually / go / walk / in the morning.
What did you do last weekend?	go / a wedding.

natural English link words and phrases

2 Read the texts. Underline five more link words or phrases which tell us the order of events.

What did you do on your birthday?

<u>First of all</u> I met some friends after work in a bar. We had a couple of drinks together and then we went to a restaurant for a meal. Afterwards we went to a club.

*What did you do on **New Year's Eve** last year?*

First we went to my uncle's house for a family dinner. After that we went to a friend's house for an hour or so. Then we went to the town square where we watched the fireworks.

New Year's Eve December 31st

write it!

You are writing a letter or e-mail to a friend. Write about last New Year's Eve <u>or</u> your last birthday.

wordbooster

irregular verbs

3 Order the sentences in the story.

a ☐ <u>started</u> ✓ chasing the thief and <u>bited</u> *bit* ✗ him!

b ☐ The guy <u>thrown</u> my bag down on the ground and tried to run

c ☐ chased him into a park. Zac <u>fell</u> and <u>hurted</u> himself but then a dog

d ☐ *1* I <u>were</u> in a café with my boyfriend Zac. We were having a coffee when

e ☐ Zac <u>run</u> after him and

f ☐ So in the end I <u>got</u> my bag back but Zac <u>breaked</u> his arm!

g ☐ away but Zac finally <u>catched</u> him.

h ☐ suddenly this guy <u>stealed</u> my bag and <u>rushed</u> out of the café.

Look at the underlined verbs in the past simple. Are they right ✓ or wrong ✗? Correct the wrong ones.

say it!

Look at the pictures and re-tell the story.
Now remember the <u>past participles</u> of the underlined verbs.

phrasal verbs (2)

4 Match the beginnings and endings of the sentences.

His arm hurt but he carried	a up when the teacher came in.
1 Our bus broke	b off early tomorrow morning.
2 The flight took	c on working.
3 We're going to set	d off three hours late.
4 I lay	e over and cut my leg.
5 At school we had to stand	f down on the sofa and fell asleep.
6 He turned	g away when the man shouted.
7 I fell	h down on the motorway.
8 The children ran	i up late for work again today.

expand your vocabulary

synonyms

Read these two versions of the same story. The meaning is similar but the underlined verbs in the second story are more descriptive.

A guy <u>took</u> my bag, <u>quickly walked</u> out of the café and <u>ran</u> down the street. I <u>shouted</u> at him to stop and the waiter <u>ran after</u> him. He caught him but the thief <u>hit</u> him and <u>broke</u> his glasses. Then suddenly a dog appeared and <u>bit</u> him so he <u>threw</u> my bag down on the ground.

A guy <u>grabbed</u> my bag, <u>rushed</u> out of the café and <u>sprinted</u> down the street. I <u>yelled</u> at him to stop and the waiter <u>chased</u> him. He caught him but the thief <u>punched</u> him and <u>smashed</u> his glasses. Then suddenly a dog appeared and <u>attacked</u> him so he <u>chucked</u> my bag down on the ground.

Read the second story again and match the underlined verbs with the definitions 1 to 8.

	move quickly to get somewhere or do sth	*rush*
1	hit using a closed hand	_____
2	try to hurt sb	_____
3	take sth suddenly or quickly	_____
4	run very quickly	_____
5	throw sth not in a careful way	_____
6	shout loudly	_____
7	run after sb	_____
8	break into many pieces	_____

test yourself!

Cover the second story. Retell the first story using the other verbs.

A guy ~~took~~ grabbed my bag ...

---

we had a terrible time

natural English *have a good / bad time*

5   Order the words to make sentences. The first word is underlined.

A   Does your brother like Spain?
B   having / <u>I</u> / a / time / think / 's / great / he
   I think he's having a great time.

1   A   Was your holiday good?
    B   we / <u>No</u> / time / terrible / had / a
    _____

2   A   Is your sister enjoying herself in Canada?
    B   good / 's / a / not / <u>She</u> / time / having
    _____

3   A   I went to stay with my relatives for New Year.
    B   have / a / time / good / you / <u>Did</u> ?
    _____

4   A   Let's go home now.
    B   having / a / <u>Why</u>? / / I / time / 'm / great
    _____

5   A   I'm going out now.
    B   <u>Have</u> / time / good / a
    _____

6   A   Did Harry enjoy the trip?
    B   a / didn't / good / he / time / have / <u>No</u>
    _____

7   A   How was the party?
    B   great / <u>I</u> / a / had / time
    _____

8   A   time / having / you / <u>Are</u> / good / a ?
    _____
    B   Yes. I'm really enjoying it.

say it!

Respond to these sentences.

Is your sister enjoying university?	She's ...
Was the party good?	I had ...
I went to a club last night.	Did you ...
I'm going on holiday tomorrow.	Have a ...
Why did Alex go home?	He wasn't ...

She's having a great time.

natural English uses of get

6 Complete the sentences using words from the box.

a high mark	London	my e-mail	a CD player	a prize
work	the cinema	~~home~~	here	

I'm so tired. I got _home_ at 3 a.m. last night.

1 Did you get _____ ? I sent it this morning.

2 We got to _____ at 7.30 p.m. and missed the beginning of the film.

3 I didn't get _____ in the test.

4 If we leave at 7 a.m., we'll get to _____ by 10.

5 I have to get to _____ by 8 a.m. when I start my new job.

6 She got _____ for the best exam results in her school.

7 I got _____ for my birthday.

8 **A** Have you been waiting long?

B No, I only got _____ five minutes ago.

grammar past simple and past continuous

7 Underline the correct form, past simple or past continuous.

how we met

Rachael and Jason

I had / <u>was having</u> a day off work. I ¹ walked / was walking down the street when a girl in front of me ² dropped / was dropping her bag. All of her shopping ³ fell / was falling out, so I ⁴ helped / was helping her pick it up. That's how I met Rachael.

Marta and Jakub

I ⁵ sat / was sitting at my desk at work one day when Jakub ⁶ arrived / was arriving. It was his first day at work and he ⁷ wore / was wearing jeans which my boss hates! I liked him immediately and six months later we ⁸ got / were getting married!

Charlotte and Pascal

Charlotte and I are from the same town in France but we ⁹ met / were meeting when we ¹⁰ studied / were studying English in London.

8 Make sentences in the past using the words given. You will need to add *when*.

I / work / on the computer / the power / go off.
I was working on the computer when the power went off.

I / hurt / leg / I / play basketball
I hurt my leg when I was playing basketball.

1 We / meet / I / live / in France.
_____

2 I / drive home / my car / break down.
_____

3 I / see her / I / walk / to work.
_____

4 I / do / my homework / Frederick / turn up.
_____

5 What / you / do / I / phone / you this morning?
_____

6 I / burn / my hand / I / cook / dinner.
_____

7 We / travel / in India / my sister / get sick.
_____

8 I / fall over / I / run / for the bus.
_____

say it!

Look at the photographs of the three couples again. Explain how they met.

Talk about how you met your boyfriend / girlfriend or how your parents met.

natural English asking how to say things

9 Complete the questions.

What's this _____ in English?

How do you _____ *ladrillo* in English?

Look at these pictures and write the words from unit seven.

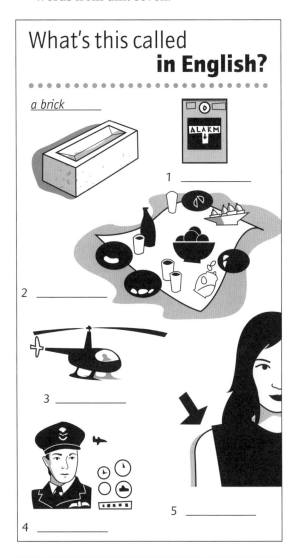

What's this called in English?

a brick _____

1 _____

2 _____

3 _____

4 _____

5 _____

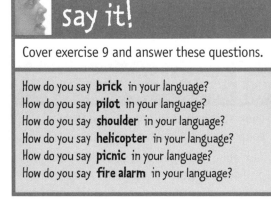
 **expand** your grammar

past continuous with *while*

> **We can use *when* or *while* to link the past simple and past continuous.**
> We <u>met</u> *when / while* I <u>was working</u> in Japan.
>
> **However, when we link two actions in the past continuous we usually use *while*. These two long actions happened <u>at the same time</u>.**

While one boy <u>was talking</u> to the woman, his brother <u>was taking</u> apples from her garden.

```
                one boy was talking
         xxxxxxxxx
past ——————————————————— now
         xxxxxxxxx
         his brother was taking apples
```

Complete the sentences using the verbs in brackets in the past continuous.

While he *was talking* (talk) on his mobile, I *was doing* (do) all the work!

1 The other students _____ (make) a lot of noise while we _____ (do) the test.

2 The car _____ (make) a funny noise while we _____ (drive) here.

3 They _____ (talk) while I _____ (watch) TV.

4 While I _____ (live) in New York , I _____ (do) three jobs to make enough money.

5 _____ (you / listen) to me while I _____ (talk) to you?

6 What _____ (you / do) while I _____ (work) this morning?

7 My sister _____ (go out with) him, while he _____ (see) another girl.

8 My neighbours _____ (have) a party while I _____ (try) to sleep.

Tick (✓) when you've done these sections.

natural English
- ☐ suggestions
- ☐ *all day / night / week / the time*
- ☐ invitations
- ☐ making arrangements

grammar
- ☐ *be going to / might / would like to*
- ☐ present continuous for future
- ☐ expand your grammar present simple for events on a timetable

vocabulary
- ☐ time phrases
- ☐ verb + noun collocation
- ☐ expand your vocabulary expressions with *have*

free time

natural English suggestions

1 Rosanna is talking to Jenny about how to celebrate Jenny's birthday. Write Rosanna's suggestions using the words given.

	Rosanna	have a party (could)
		You could have a party.
1	Rosanna	go to a club (what)
		_____
	Jenny	I don't like clubs very much.
2	Rosanna	have a picnic in the park (could)
		_____
	Jenny	Hmm, maybe.
3	Rosanna	get tickets for a show (how)
		_____
	Jenny	Hmm, that could be expensive.
4	Rosanna	go out for a meal (how)
		_____
	Jenny	Yeah, good idea.
5	Rosanna	go away for the weekend (what)
		_____
	Jenny	Yeah, lovely.

 **say it!**

> You could have a party.

> How about having a party?

pronunciation Remember the intonation and sentence stress. Practise Rosanna's suggestions in exercise 1.

You and a friend are talking about what to do this afternoon. Make suggestions using the pictures.

CINEMA

> We could go and see a film.

grammar *be going to / might / would like to*

2 Tick ✓ the best sentence.

I might have to work on Saturday.
a   I start at 7 a.m.
b   My boss is going to call me this afternoon. ✓

1   They're going to call the baby Elizabeth.
a   That's her grandmother's name.
b   Claire can't decide.

2   I'd like to go to the Eminem concert.
a   I got one of the last tickets.
b   But I think they've sold all the tickets.

3   I might study tourism at college.
a   I haven't decided yet.
b   My course starts on Monday.

4   I'd like to go to America.
a   Maybe next year I will.
b   I've just bought my ticket.

5   My parents are going to sell our house.
a   But mum's not really sure yet.
b   They've already found a place they want to buy.

3 Some university students are talking about their plans for the summer holidays. Complete the sentences using *be going to, might,* or *would like to*. Use the verbs given.

I *'d like to get* (get) a job as tour guide for the summer but I think it'll be difficult.

1   I _____ (work) as an **au pair** in Spain for three months. I'm really excited about it.

2   I _____ (have) a holiday but I can't. I've got to work for my dad.

3   My parents are going to Europe on holiday so I _____ (go) with them. I'm not sure yet.

4   Some of my friends are going on holiday together. I _____ (go) but I don't have enough money.

5   My sister and I _____ (stay) with our relatives in the country for three weeks. We go there every year.

au pair /ˌaʊˈpeə/ (n) a foreigner who lives with a family and helps to take care of the children and sometimes does housework.

wordbooster

time phrases

4 Match the beginnings and endings of the sentences.

|c| I'm meeting him
1   ☐ What did you do last
2   ☐ I've got classes all tomorrow
3   ☐ We're going on holiday the day
4   ☐ What are you doing
5   ☐ I'm taking my exams in
6   ☐ I'm going to see the dentist next
7   ☐ I saw her the day before
8   ☐ He went to the doctor two days

a   eight days' time.
b   ago.
c   ~~this Friday.~~
d   after tomorrow.
e   night?
f   Tuesday.
g   yesterday.
h   tonight?
i   morning.

say it!

Sun	Mon	Tues	Wed	Thurs	Fri	Sat
8	9	10	11	12	13	14
	a			b		c
15	16	17	18	19	20	21
	today		d			
22	23	24	25	26	27	28
e				f		

What do we call days a to f? When possible think of two different ways of saying it.

a last Monday or a week ago

expand your vocabulary

expressions with *have*

Read the text and add the underlined words to the diagram.

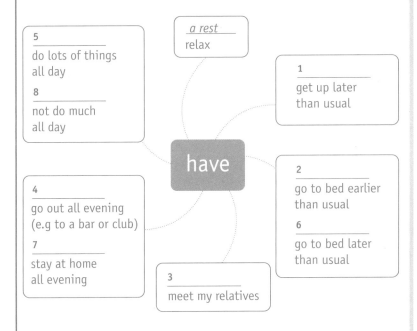

```
5 _____          a rest          1 _____
do lots of things         relax           get up later
all day                                   than usual
8 _____
not do much                    have
all day                                   2 _____
                                          go to bed earlier
4 _____                          than usual
go out all evening                        6 _____
(e.g to a bar or club)                    go to bed later
7 _____                          than usual
stay at home
all evening               3 _____
                          meet my relatives
```

Add these expressions. They are the opposites of three expressions in the diagram.

a late night   a quiet day   a night in

Complete the sentences using the words above.

I *had a late night* yesterday so I'm going to go to bed early tonight.

1   I'm going to _____ on Saturday. It's my friend's birthday party.

2   We're going to _____ to celebrate mum and dad's wedding anniversary.

3   Don't wake me until 10 a.m. I'd like to _____ .

4   I'm going to _____ this afternoon before we go out.

5   I'm going to _____ tonight. I'm so tired!

6   **A**   Did you _____ at work?
    B   Yes! I couldn't even stop for lunch!

7   **A**   Are you going out this evening?
    B   No! I'm going to _____ and just watch TV.

8   We _____ in the shop. In fact there were only five customers all day!

write it!

Write a magazine article (like the one above) about your Sunday.

My Sunday

■ **How do you start the day?**
I always have <u>a night out</u> on Saturday, so on Sunday I have <u>a lie-in</u> until about 9.30 or 10. Then I have a coffee in bed and read.

■ **Lazy or active?**
Definitely lazy! I usually have <u>a very busy day</u> on Saturday and then on Sunday I have <u>a rest</u>. I don't play any sport or anything like that.

■ **Friends or family?**
I often see friends in the afternoon. We go to a movie or watch a match. Once a month we have <u>a family get-together</u> and my mum cooks a big Sunday lunch.

■ **Sunday night – in or out?**
Sometimes I go round to a friend's house and we watch a DVD. Or if I stay at home then I make a few phone calls and have <u>an early night.</u>

natural English *all day / night / week / the time*

5   Make new sentences with the same meanings. Replace the words in colour with *all day / all night / all week / all the time*.

I've always got my mobile with me.
I've got my mobile with me all the time .

1   Yoshiaki had to work from 9 p.m. to 6 a.m.

    _____

2   It rained from Monday to Sunday.

    _____

3   I have to study from morning to evening on Saturday.

    _____

4   I always feel tired.

    _____

5   She was in the meeting from 9 a.m. to 5 p.m.

how to ... make arrangements

vocabulary verb + noun collocation

think back!

Remember which verbs and nouns go together.

| 1 | accept <br> make <br> invite <br> refuse <br> book | 2 | a booking <br> arrangements <br> friends for dinner <br> an invitation <br> an appointment <br> plans <br> a table |

6 Read the quiz and tick your answers. Then underline the verb and noun collocations from the think back! box.

Are you **always** honest?

1 A good friend has invited you to her wedding. Your ex-boyfriend / girlfriend is going to the wedding and you don't want to see them. Do you …

a) *accept the invitation?*
b) *refuse and say that you've already made other plans?*
c) *refuse the invitation and explain why?*

2 You're having a party in your apartment. You have only invited three people from your office because your apartment is small. A girl at work, who you haven't invited, hears you talking on the phone about the party. Do you …

a) *invite her to the party?*
b) *say nothing?*
c) *tell her about the party and explain why you can't invite her?*

3 You have a job interview next week but you haven't told your boss that you are looking for a new job. Do you …

a) *tell your boss that you have made a dentist's appointment for that day?*
b) *call work and say that you are sick on the day of the interview?*
c) *tell your boss the truth?*

4 Your girlfriend's / boyfriend's parents want to meet your parents. Both fathers have very strong opinions and you don't think they'll like each other. Do you …

a) *invite them for dinner at your house anyway?*
b) *book a table in a noisy restaurant where it's difficult to talk?*
c) *tell them that your parents are on holiday at the moment?*

5 Your boss wants you to work this weekend but you don't want to. Do you …

a) *tell him that you've already made arrangements for the weekend?*
b) *explain why you don't want to work?*
c) *go to work anyway?*

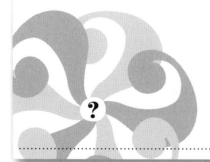

natural English invitations

7 Complete the invitations using a suitable verb.

Would *you like to come* _____ to a party with me?

1 Do _____ tennis this weekend?

2 Would _____ for a drink tomorrow evening?

3 Do _____ for a coffee after work?

4 Would _____ dinner with us on Saturday night?

5 Do _____ to the cinema tonight?

What do you say? Complete the sentences.

1 You want to accept an invitation.
Yes great, I _____ .

2 You have to refuse an invitation.
I'd love to, but _____ .

say it!

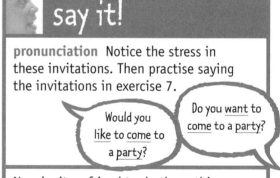

pronunciation Notice the stress in these invitations. Then practise saying the invitations in exercise 7.

Would you like to come to a party?

Do you want to come to a party?

Now invite a friend to do these things. Use a suitable verb.

the beach

a concert

a DVD

lunch

natural English making arrangements

8 Put sentences a to f into the conversation.

Carla	What are you doing on Saturday night?
Joe	___f___
Carla	Do you want to come to a party with me?
Joe	___1___
Carla	A friend of mine – Hannah. It's her birthday.
Joe	___2___
Carla	Around 8.
Joe	___3___
Carla	OK. Where shall we go?
Joe	___4___
Carla	Sounds good. Shall we meet about 6.30?
Joe	___5___

a   I'd love to. Whose party is it?

b   Why don't we go and get something to eat first?

c   What time does it start?

d   How about the pizza place near the train station?

e   OK. I'll see you there.

f   ~~Nothing, why?~~

grammar present continuous for future

9 Write sentences using the words given. Use the present continuous in each sentence.

Michael / have / a party on Saturday night.
Michael's having a party on Saturday night.

1   I / not / do / anything tomorrow night.

_____

2   you / come / to the concert next Friday?

_____

3   I / play / volleyball this afternoon.

_____

4   We / meet / at 6 o'clock.

_____

5   My parents / have / a dinner party tonight.

_____

6   What / you / do / this weekend?

_____

7   My sister / stay / at a friend's house all weekend.

_____

8   Where / you / have / dinner?

_____

expand your grammar

present simple for events on a timetable

Notice the tense of the verbs in these sentences.
What time <u>does</u> the next train <u>leave</u>?
The film <u>starts</u> at 8.30.
My bus <u>goes</u> at 7.45.
When <u>is</u> your flight?

The present simple is used to talk about future events when these are scheduled or on a timetable.
The train leaves at 10.00 a.m. = This train leaves at this time every day.

When the arrangement is personal the present continuous is used.
The film <u>starts</u> at 8.30 but we'<u>re meeting</u> at 8.00 for a coffee first.

Complete the sentences using the verbs in the present simple or the present continuous.

The new sports centre *opens* (open) next Friday.

I *'m playing* (play) tennis this afternoon.

1   What time _____ ? (the concert / start)

2   What time _____ Jane? (you / meet)

3   My class _____ (finish) at 4.30. I can meet you then.

4   I _____ (have) dinner with some friends tonight.

5   My flight _____ (be) at 10.30 so I should get to the airport by 9.

6   Are you ready? The bus _____ (go) at 7.45.

7   We _____ (go) to the cinema later. Why don't you come?

8   My course _____ (begin) on September 5th.

Tick (✓) when you've done these sections.

natural English
- [ ] *still*
- [ ] use of *long*
- [ ] *there's ... / there are ..., it's got ...*
- [ ] vague language: *thing(s)*

grammar
- [ ] present perfect with *for* and *since*
- [ ] *should / shouldn't*
- [ ] expand your grammar *everybody / somebody / nobody / anybody*

vocabulary
- [ ] homes
- [ ] adjectives describing homes
- [ ] expand your vocabulary compound nouns

life changes

natural English *still*

1 Grace and Marianne are friends but they haven't seen each other for two years. They meet again at a party.

Grace remembers these things about Marianne's life two years ago. Write her questions using *still*.

    She lived in London.   *Do you still live in London*_____ ?

1 She worked in advertising. _____ ?

2 She played a lot of tennis. _____ ?

3 She was friends with Chloe. _____ ?

4 Her brother sang in a band. _____ ?

5 She was going out with Charlie. _____ ?

2 Grace tells Marianne about herself. Order the words to make sentences. The first word is underlined.

    work / in / post office / <u>I</u> / part-time / the / still
    *I still work part-time in the post office.*_____

1 with / still / parents / <u>I</u> / live / my

    _____

2 still / university / <u>I</u> / at / am

    _____

3 Spain / lives / sister / in / <u>My</u> / still

    _____

4 want / a / be / <u>I</u> / still / writer / to

    _____

5 Vanessa / am / <u>I</u> / with / still / friends

    _____

say it!

Look at the sentences in exercise 2.
Ask questions using *still*.

> Do you still work part-time in the post office?

grammar present perfect with *for* and *since*

3 Tick ✓ the possible endings for these sentences. One or two endings may be possible.

She's worked here since
a 1997. ✓
b 8 years.
c she left college. ✓

1 They've been married for
a a long time.
b 1980.
c 25 years.

2 I haven't seen her since
a your sister's wedding.
b 6 months.
c 2 years.

3 My brother has lived in New York for
a about 5 years.
b a few years.
c 1999.

4 I've known Rob since
a we were at primary school.
b 1990.
c 15 years.

5 I've only had this car for
a my 18th birthday.
b 6 months.
c last May.

say it!

pronunciation Remember to use the weak pronunciation of *for* /fə/. Notice the linking of *for* before a vowel sound.

for_eight days /fəreɪt/ for_a month /fərəmʌnθ/

Practise saying these phrases.

for 5 years	for 3 weeks	for 2 hours
for 6 months	for a year	for a month
for a long time	for about a week	

4 Read the e-mail. Put the verbs into the present simple, past simple, or present perfect.

Dear James,

It _was_ (be) great to hear from you again.

I can't believe we 1 _____ (not / see)

each other for three years! Congratulations on your wedding and I'm sorry

that I couldn't come. Where 2 _____ (you / live) now? I 3 _____

(move) into an apartment with some friends six months ago. I 4 _____

(work) for an IT company. I 5 _____ (be) there since we left college.

What about you? 6 _____ (you / still / work) for the

bank? By the way, I've got a new girlfriend called Linda. We 7 _____ (be)

together for about three months. Actually, we 8 _____ (know) each other

since we were about ten years old but we only started going out together

in June.

Let's keep in touch now. I'd love to see you again.

Tim

write it!

Write a similar e-mail about yourself to a friend you haven't seen for two or three years.

natural English use of *long*

5 Match the questions and answers.

Have you lived here long?

1 Have you had that jacket long?
2 Have you been here long?
3 Have they been married long?
4 Has he worked here long?
5 Have you worn **contact lenses** long?
6 Have they known each other long?
7 Has he had that car long?
8 Has your sister been in France long?

a I've just arrived.
b His parents gave it to him for his last birthday.
c They've been friends for years.
d We moved here when I was 15.
e It's their fifth wedding anniversary this week.
f I bought it last week.
g Since I was 18 but I wore glasses before that.
h She went there about six months ago.
i No. It's his first day.

contact lenses /ˈkɒntækt ˈlenzɪz/ (n) small, round, thin pieces of plastic you put on your eyes to make you see better

wordbooster

homes

think back!

Remember five more rooms in a house. *kitchen*

6 Do the crossword.

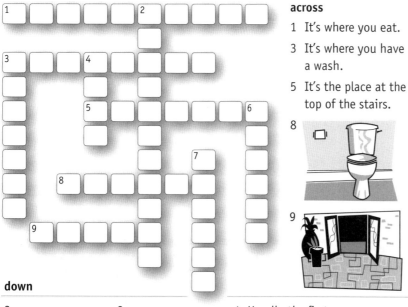

across

1 It's where you eat.

3 It's where you have a wash.

5 It's the place at the top of the stairs.

8

9

down

4 Usually the first room you enter in a house.

6 It's where you park your car.

7

adjectives describing homes

7 One adjective in each sentence is wrong. Correct it using a word from the box.

cold	spacious	~~old~~	untidy	modern	dark

  old
The apartment building is ~~new~~. It was built a hundred years ago.

1 Their house is very light. They need the lights on all day.

2 His room is always so tidy. He never puts anything away.

3 It's a very traditional building. I think it was built a year ago.

4 The apartment is very small. There are five bedrooms, a huge kitchen, and a big living room.

5 My apartment is really warm in the winter. I always have to wear a jumper.

natural English *there's… / there are…, it's got …*

8 You want to go to a fitness centre. Look at these three centres, Healthworks (H), Fitness One (FO), and Solo Gym (SG).

	H	FO	SG
a swimming pool	✓	✓	✓
1 a sauna	✓		✓
2 a gym	✓	✓	✓
3 a yoga studio		✓	
4 a café	✓(2)		✓
5 a car park			✓ (2)

Write sentences about Healthworks fitness centre.

> *It's got a swimming pool.*
> *There's a swimming pool.*

1 It _____

2 There _____

3 It _____

4 There _____

5 It _____

Write questions and short answers about Fitness One.

> *Has it got a swimming pool?*
> *Yes, it has.*
> *Is there a swimming pool?*
> *Yes, there is.*

1 Has _____
_____

2 Is _____
_____

3 Has _____
_____

4 Is _____
_____

5 Has _____
_____

say it!

Talk about Solo Gym.

There's a swimming pool.

 # expand your vocabulary

compound nouns

> **Many words in English are made from two nouns.**
>
> **noun + noun**
>
> car park   bedroom   ground floor
>
> **pronunciation** The stress is usually on the first word, e.g. <u>din</u>ing room, <u>car</u> park.

Name the things in the pictures using one word from each box.

A	arm	computer	~~DVD~~	light	fire
	front	key	video	kitchen	

B	camera	desk	place	cupboard	door
	switch	ring	~~player~~	chair	

DVD player

1 _____

2 _____

3 _____

4 _____

5 _____

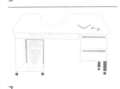

6 _____

7 _____

8 _____

test yourself!

Look at the pictures and name the things.

 # how to... give opinions

grammar _should / shouldn't_

9 Read the magazine article.

Job interviews

Job interviews can be difficult. Follow some simple advice and you won't go wrong.

- Ask some questions about the company and the job but not too many. This is just the first interview. You can get all the details later.
- Make sure that you answer all the questions they ask you. If you didn't understand something, ask them to repeat it.
- Be honest! If you lie about something and you get the job somebody will find out the truth.
- You can talk about jobs you've had, but it's not a good idea to give information about the companies you've worked for before.
- It's OK to ask about the **salary**, but wait until the end of the interview.
- Look clean and smart. You can be fashionable but not too **unusual**.

> **salary** /ˈsæləri/ (n) the money that you earn
>
> **unusual** /ʌnˈjuːʒuəl/ (adj) different or strange

What advice does the writer give? Write _should_ or _shouldn't_.

You _shouldn't_ ask a lot of questions.

1 You _____ answer all the questions they ask you.

2 You _____ always tell the truth.

3 You _____ talk about other companies you've worked for.

4 You _____ ask about money at the beginning of the interview.

5 You _____ dress well.

say it!

A friend has a job interview tomorrow. Give him advice using these ideas and _should_ or _shouldn't_. Then add your own ideas.

find out about the company before you go
take a taxi and arrive on time
talk too much
take your **CV** with you

> You should find out about the company before you go.

> **CV (curriculum vitae)** /ˈsiː.viː/ (n) a document which lists your personal information, education, and previous jobs

natural English vague language: *thing(s)*

10 Put sentences a to f into the conversations.

A Have you got another meeting with Mr. Jones tomorrow?

B __f__

1 **A** Are you coming for a coffee?

B _____

2 **A** _____

B Like what?

A He doesn't listen and he's always late.

3 **A** He suddenly stood up and ran out of the room.

B _____

4 **A** Do you like the apartment?

B _____

5 **A** _____

B This?

A No, the plastic thing.

a I can't. I've got a lot of things to do this afternoon.

b That was a strange thing to do.

c He does a lot of things which make me cross.

d The best thing about it is the view.

e Can you give me that thing over there?

f ~~Yes. We've still got some things to talk about.~~

expand your grammar

everybody / somebody / nobody / anybody

every_____ means 100%	some_____ means 1	no_____ means 0	any_____ is usually used in questions and negatives
everybody* everywhere everything	somebody* somewhere something	nobody* nowhere nothing	anybody* anywhere anything + singular verb

* You can also say *everyone / someone / no one / anyone*.

Everybody / Everyone <u>likes</u> him.   Nobody / No one <u>lives</u> there.

Wait. I've forgotten something.   Have you ever lived anywhere else?

Some foreign students are talking about being in England. Underline the correct word.

I'd like to go <u>everywhere</u> / nowhere / anywhere in Europe but I don't have enough money.

1 At first I didn't know everybody / nobody / anybody here. Now I've got some friends.

2 I think everything / something / anything's quite expensive here.

3 The people are nice. On my first day I got lost, but somebody / anybody / nobody helped me.

4 When I arrived I couldn't understand something / anything / nothing. It's better now.

5 Everybody / Somebody / Nobody speaks my language here, so sometimes it's difficult for me.

6 It's really exciting being somewhere / anywhere / nowhere new.

7 Everybody / Anybody / Nobody is friendly here. People talk to me all the time.

8 I didn't have everywhere / anywhere / nowhere to stay when I arrived, but I found a room easily.

ten   how do you feel?

Tick (✓) when you've done these sections.

natural English
- [ ] accepting and refusing suggestions
- [ ] fillers in conversation

grammar
- [ ] −ed/−ing adjectives
- [ ] verb patterns
- [ ] expand your grammar
      had ('d) better + verb

vocabulary
- [ ] sleep
- [ ] aches and pains
- [ ] expand your vocabulary health

 **sleepwalking**

vocabulary sleep

1   Each of the questions has one word missing. Write the missing word in each question.

Can you remember your dreams when you wake *up*?

1   What time do you usually go bed?

2   Do you find it difficult to asleep?

3   Do you talk your sleep?

4   Do noises in the night wake up easily?

5   Do you ever nightmares?

Match the questions and answers.

a _____ When I was younger I sometimes dreamt about having an accident.

b _____ I sometimes can't get to sleep for a long time – especially if I'm thinking about work.

c *example* If I wake up during the night I remember them, but in the morning I don't.

d _____ Between 10 p.m. and 11 p.m. I need eight hours' sleep every night.

e _____ Yes, I'm a light sleeper. If a car drives past in the night I wake up!

f _____ My sister says that when we shared a room she sometimes heard me talking but she couldn't understand me.

say it!

Answers questions 1 to 5 for yourself.

grammar -ed/-ing adjectives

2 Complete the sentences using *be + very/ really* and *-ed/-ing* adjectives from the box.

frightened/ing	surprised/ing	bored/ing
interested/ing	~~annoyed/ing~~	embarrassed/ing
worried/ying	relaxed/ing	excited/ing

I had to wait 35 minutes for the bus and then I couldn't get a seat.
It *was really annoying.*

1 I went to the job interview wearing one black and one brown shoe.
I _____ .

2 I had an eight-hour bus journey.
It _____ .

3 Carlos is going on holiday tomorrow.
He _____ .

4 Leila's dad's in hospital.
She _____ .

5 I watched a great documentary last night.
It _____ .

6 We were lost and it was starting to get dark.
It _____ .

7 My sister didn't expect to pass her exams but she did.
She _____ .

8 I was at the beach all day.
It _____ .

say it!

It was really annoying.

pronunciation
Underline the stressed syllables in the adjectives in the box. Practise saying the sentences in exercise 2.

3 Some students have written stories for a school magazine. Match the stories and the titles.

a My most **embarrassing** experience.

b The most **exciting** thing I've ever done.

c The most **frightening** thing that's ever happened to me.

1 _____ **Antonio, Italy**

*I was skiing with some friends. We were on the mountain when there was a really loud noise. It sounded like a gun. I looked up and saw a wall of snow coming towards us. It was an **avalanche**. Everyone was screaming and started to ski down the mountain, but the avalanche was too quick. Suddenly I was underneath snow and I couldn't see anything.*

2 _____ **Carina, Denmark**

It was my first day as a teacher. I went to my new classroom and introduced myself. I started teaching but then a man walked into the room. I thought he was a student and I asked him to sit down. Then some of the students started laughing. The man told me that I was in the wrong classroom. This was the teacher and this was his class. My students were in the room next door!

3 _____ **Jonathon, USA**

I went on a three-week adventure holiday in the Himalayas. There was a group of 12 of us. We met our guide in Katmandu and then took a tiny plane up to one of the mountain villages. It was amazing. Every day we walked from village to village through the mountains. It was very tiring but the views and the people we met were fantastic.

avalanche /ˈævəlɑːnʃ/ (n) when a lot of snow falls down a mountain

 write it!

Choose one of the titles and write your own magazine story.

wordbooster

aches and pains

think back!

Remember five more words for aches and pains. *headache*

4 Order the words to make sentences.

A leg / pain / I / in / got / a / my / 've
I've got a pain in my leg.

B go / the / to / you / doctor / should
You should go to the doctor.

1 A matter / 's / what / the / ?
_____

B my / hurts / arm
_____

2 A 's / wrong / what?
_____

B in / 've / a / foot / got / I / terrible / my / pain
_____

3 A sick / feel / I
_____

B water / like / you / would / some ?
_____

4 A headache / I / a / 've / got
_____

B some / you / tablets / I / get / 'll
_____

5 A feel / don't / well / I
_____

B home / you / why / go / don't ?
_____

say it!

Answer this question using the words given.

> I've got stomachache.

What's the matter?
stomach   pain / leg   back / hurt   tooth   sick

---

expand your vocabulary

health

Match the pictures and the words.

a   b   c

d   e

a runny nose	*d*
1 a cut	_____
2 a temperature /ˈtemprətʃə/	_____
3 a sore throat /sɔː ˈθrəʊt/	_____
4 sunburn /ˈsʌnbɜːn/	_____

Complete the sentences with the words below.

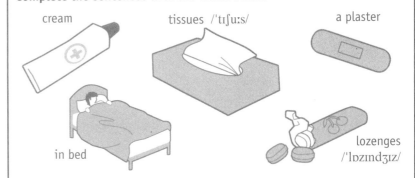

cream   tissues /ˈtɪʃuːs/   a plaster

in bed   lozenges /ˈlɒzɪndʒɪz/

A I've got a sore throat.   **B** You should get some *lozenges.*

1 A I've cut my finger.   **B** Do you want _____?

2 A I've got a temperature.   **B** You should be _____.

3 A I've got a runny nose.   **B** Need some _____?

4 A I've got sunburn.   **B** Use some of this _____.

test yourself!

Look at the pictures and say the words.

how to ... make an appointment

grammar verb patterns

5 Cross out *to* if it is wrong.

He sent ~~to~~ her some flowers.

1 Don't forget to phone to your dad.
2 Did you thank to Justyna for the present?
3 I spoke to Pataraporn this morning.
4 Did you e-mail to Louise?
5 I sent to him a text message.
6 I wrote to them.
7 Why didn't you ask to me?
8 I didn't tell to Aidan anything.

6 Write sentences using *I have to* and the words given. You may need to add *to*.

write / Megumi

I have to write to Megumi.

1 e-mail / Pedro

_____

2 phone / the doctor

_____

3 speak / Barbara

_____

4 thank / Sid / for the flowers

_____

5 talk / Pierre

_____

6 ring / Delphine

_____

7 ask / Fiona / for her class notes

_____

8 send text message / Mirko

_____

natural English accepting and refusing suggestions

7 Complete the conversations using the words given in brackets.

A I'd like to talk about this again.
B *What about tomorrow morning?*
   SUGGEST TOMORROW MORNING (what)
A 1 _____
   REFUSE (afraid)

A When shall we meet?
B 2 _____
   SUGGEST TUESDAY (how)
A 3 _____
   ACCEPT (great)

A Dr Brown can see you at 10 a.m. on Wednesday.
B 4 _____
   REFUSE (no good)

A The next appointment is Friday at 9.30 a.m.
B 5 _____
   ACCEPT (fine)

say it!

Accept or refuse the invitations and suggestions.

What about meeting tomorrow morning?
REFUSE

I'm afraid I can't.

a
How about Saturday morning?
REFUSE
How about Saturday afternoon?
ACCEPT

b
You can see Dr Brown at 2 p.m.
REFUSE
What about 3 p.m.?
ACCEPT

natural English fillers in conversation

8 Complete the conversation with the sentences below.

Just here.

No, never.

Well, I've got really bad stomachache.

~~Hello. I'm Susie.~~

Hmmm, for about three days.

Let me see, er, I had some toast for breakfast. That's all.

Doctor	Hello, I'm Doctor Marshall.
Susie	*Hello. I 'm Susie.*
Doctor	What's the matter?
Susie	1 _____
Doctor	Have you had it for long?
Susie	2 _____
Doctor	OK. Now, tell me exactly where it hurts.
Susie	3 _____
Doctor	Right. Have you eaten anything today?
Susie	4 _____
Doctor	Have you had a pain like this before?
Susie	5 _____
Doctor	I'll have a look, but don't worry. I'm sure it's not serious.

Find four more *fillers* in the conversation.

Well _____ , *OK* _____ , _____ ,

_____ , _____ , _____ .

> **fillers** / ˈfɪləz / (n) words which help to make the conversation more natural

expand your grammar

had ('d) better + verb

> **Had better** usually means *should* for <u>specific situations</u>.
> **A** I feel sick.
> **B** You**'d better** lie down. = You should / It's a good idea to lie down.
> I**'d better** go home now. It's getting late.
> We**'d better** meet in the car park.
> They**'d better** hurry up. The bus will be here soon.
>
> For <u>general situations</u> only use *should*.
> Everyone **should** learn a second language. ✓
> Everyone ~~had better~~ learn a second language. ✗

Underline the correct word or words. (Both words may be possible.)

You <u>*'d better*</u> / <u>*should*</u> say sorry to her. She's really upset.

1 We 'd better / should set off early. It's a long way.

2 People had better / should vote in elections.

3 You 'd better / should take a jacket. It'll be cold tonight.

4 Your dad had better / should make a booking at the restaurant. It's always busy.

5 Teachers had better / should be paid more money.

Complete the sentences using '*d better* and the phrases from the box.

~~go to class~~	phone her	go to the dentist
look again	buy tickets today	set my alarm clock

   A It's 1 p.m.

   B I *'d better go to class.*

1 **A** I've got toothache again.

   B You _____ .

2 **A** Julia didn't come to school today.

   B I _____ .

3 **A** Some of my friends want to come to the concert too.

   B They _____ .

4 **A** I can't find my passport.

   B You _____ .

5 **A** We're going to set off at about 6 a.m.

   B I _____ .

eleven

Tick (✓) when you've done these sections.

natural English
☐ leaving out words
☐ *I (don't) agree / it depends*
☐ uses of *work* (n)
☐ *What if ...?*

grammar
☐ conditional sentences with *will / might*
☐ expand your grammar ellipsis

vocabulary
☐ work and working conditions
☐ office jobs
☐ relationships
☐ expand your vocabulary computers

how to ...
describe office life

natural English leaving out words

1 Which words can be left out in natural, spoken English? Put them in brackets.

> (Have you) had a busy day? OR
> (Have you had a) busy day?

1 Do you need some help?
2 Are you hungry?
3 I don't think so.
4 Did you have a good time?
5 Have you got any change?
6 Are you OK?
7 Would you like a coffee?
8 I'll tell you later.

Complete the conversations using the sentences above.

> A Had a busy day? / Busy day?
> B Yeah – really busy!

1 A _____?
  B No – I've just had a sandwich.

2 A _____?
  B No – I don't feel well.

3 A _____?
  B No thanks. I've had three cups this morning!

4 A _____?
  B Yeah, it was really relaxing.

5 A Is Jane coming to the party?
  B _____.

6 A _____?
  B Yes please! This is really difficult.

7 A _____?
  B Sure. How much do you need?

8 A What time will you finish today?
  B _____.

 say it!

Like a chocolate?

Say the sentences, leaving out words.

Would you like a chocolate?	Have you been here long?	I'll call you tonight.
Are you tired?	Have you got any paper?	I'll see you later.

expand your grammar

ellipsis

It is natural to leave out some words in a sentence when they repeat information.

I like working here but Peter doesn't (like working here).

Alicia passed the test but Concha didn't (pass the test).

She can't drive but I can (drive).

I'm not interested but Helen is (interested).

For verbs other than *be*, when there is no auxiliary verb you need to add one.

She doesn't work full-time but I work full-time. →

   She doesn't work full-time but I <u>do</u>.

Luca didn't go to the party but Adam went to the party. →

   Luca didn't go to the party but Adam <u>did</u>.

Make these sentences more natural by crossing out or adding words if necessary.

   I can't speak German but my friend can ~~speak German.~~

   I don't know about motorbikes but my brother ~~knows about motorbikes.~~ *does.*

1 She wasn't upset about it but he was upset about it.

2 I wanted to go home but my friends didn't want to go home.

3 I still live at home but my sister doesn't live at home.

4 David didn't like the film but I liked the film.

5 She's French but he isn't French.

6 Meg doesn't work on Saturdays but Chris works on Saturdays.

7 My flatmate can cook but I can't cook.

8 Jessica doesn't like him but I like him.

9 My dad's excited about it but my mum isn't excited about it.

10 I didn't go to the concert but Nadine went to the concert.

natural English *I (don't) agree / it depends*

JENS   **ANDY**   **JACK**

2 Three colleagues are talking about work clothes. Put these sentences into the conversations.

a I think it depends.

b I don't agree with that.

c I agree with that.

Andy It's important to feel comfortable when you're working. I think it's okay to wear casual clothes to work.

Jens ¹ _____ I think everyone should look smart for work.

Jack People should wear what they like. Clothes aren't important. What matters is how good you are at your job.

Andy ² _____ In some jobs clothes are not important but in others they are very important.

Jens People should always look smart at work. It shows that you are really serious about your job.

Andy ³ _____ When someone looks really **scruffy** I think that they don't really care about their job.

scruffy / ˈskrʌfi / (adj) untidy or old clothes

vocabulary work and working conditions

3 Read the first text then complete the second text with suitable words. The meaning should stay the same.

I really enjoy work. I'm the manager of a sports club. I work long hours. I never start at 9 and finish at 5 but I earn a lot. I'm usually very busy so I don't stop for lunch. There are five of us in the office. We have a good relationship and it's good fun.

I really enjoy my _job_. I ¹_____ a sports club.

My ²_____ are long. I never work nine

³_____ five but I get a good ⁴_____ .

I've got a lot of ⁵_____ to do so I don't usually have

a ⁶_____ . I ⁷_____ an office with five

other people. We ⁸_____ on well and it's good fun.

natural English uses of _work_ (n)

4 Match the beginnings and endings of these sentences and questions.

	Have you got a lot		a	to work?
1	How do you get		b	a suit to work.
2	I usually finish		c	work at around 5.30 p.m.
3	I have to wear		d	of work this week?
4	I've got some		e	when I was 17.
5	I started work		f	work to finish and then I'll meet you.

say it!

Answer these questions about your own job. If you don't work, imagine you are a travel agent or a teacher.

What sort of work do you do?
Where do you work?
How do you get to work?
What time do you start work?
Have you got a lot of work to do today?

> I'm a travel agent.

expand your vocabulary

computers

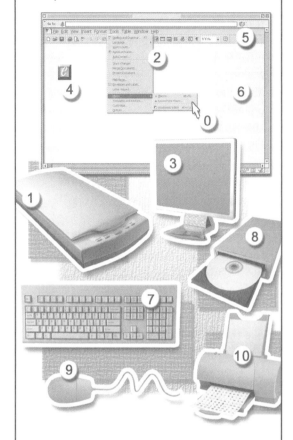

Match the things in the picture with the words in the box.

~~cursor~~	mouse	toolbar	scanner
menu	screen	icon	keyboard
monitor	printer	disk drive	

cursor

1 _____	6 _____
2 _____	7 _____
3 _____	8 _____
4 _____	9 _____
5 _____	10 _____

test yourself!

Cover the words and name the things in the picture.

wordbooster

office jobs

think back!

Remember five more office jobs. *telephonist*

5 Complete the sentences. You have the first letter of each job.

> **A** How did you get my number?
>
> **B** The t *elephonist* connected me.

1 I had an interview with the
p_____ m_____
before meeting the people in my
department.

2 When you get to the office ask the
r_____ to call me and I'll
come and meet you.

3 Speak to my s_____ and
she'll make an appointment.

4 I don't know anything about the
company finances. You need to talk to
the a_____.

5 If you want to know how many books
we sold last month you should talk to
the s_____ m_____.

say it!

Underline the stressed
syllables in the words
for office jobs.
Practise saying them.

telephonist

relationships

6 Complete the sentences with a suitable word. The meaning should stay the same.

> She wants everything that Jo has.
> She is *jealous* of Jo.

1 He argued with his girlfriend.
He had an _____ with his girlfriend.

2 They aren't going out together any more.
They've _____ up.

3 My boss is very bad at listening to people.
My boss is no _____ at listening to people.

4 My brother doesn't like doing any work!
My brother's very _____!

5 She started crying when we told her the news.
She got _____ when we told her the news.

6 Her dad's a bit frightening!
I'm _____ of her dad.

7 Is Tina Paul's girlfriend?
Is Paul going _____ with Tina?

8 He met a girl on holiday. He says he loves her.
He _____ in love with a girl he met on holiday.

can my girlfriend come too?

grammar conditional sentences with *will/might*

7 Chris has a job as a salesman but he's interested in a new job with a different company. Underline the correct word(s).

	my job now	new job
	(+)	(+)
	probably sales manager next year (more money)	company car
		no weekend work
	like the people	
		more money

Chris If I *take* / will take the new job, I ¹ get / 'll get a company car.

Mike That'll save you a lot of money.

Chris I know! Also I ² don't have to work / won't have to work at the weekends or evenings.

Mike Sounds good. But do you like the job you've got now?

Chris I like the people. If I ³ go / 'll go somewhere new, I ⁴ have to make / 'll have to make friends with everyone again.

Mike But I'm sure that won't be a problem.

Chris And if I ⁵ stay / 'll stay here, I ⁶ become / might become the sales manager next year.

Mike Really?

Chris Yes probably. And if I ⁷ become / will become the manager then I ⁸ earn / 'll earn a lot more money.

Mike It's a difficult decision.

8 Complete the sentences using the verbs given.

If you *bring* (bring) your girlfriend, you *won't talk* (not talk) to us.

1 I _____ (do) it today if I _____ (have) time.

2 If you _____ (leave) it on my desk, I _____ (look) at it later.

3 They _____ (not wait) for us if we _____ (be) late.

4 She _____ (call) you if she _____ (need) any help.

5 If you _____ (talk) to her, she _____ (listen) to you.

6 He _____ (lose) his job if he _____ (do) that again.

7 I _____ (text) you if I _____ (get) the tickets today.

8 If we _____ (not leave) soon, we _____ (miss) the train.

natural English *What if ...?*

9 Complete the conversations using *What if* and the words in the box.

it (rain)	I (fail) the exam
he (not like) the CD	I (not like) the job
they (be) late	
you (forget) to give him the message	

A *What if it rains* ?

B We'll have the party inside.

1 **A** _____

   B You can take it again next year.

2 **A** _____

   B He can take it back to the shop and change it.

3 **A** _____

   B I'm sure they'll call us.

4 **A** _____

   B You can leave.

5 **A** _____

   B Don't worry – I'll remember.

say it!

Renata is going to live in London for six months. Her sister is worried about her. Say the sentences using the words given.

(not have) enough money?	
(not get) a job?	
(not like) it there?	
(be) lonely?	
(not find) a place to live?	

What if you don't have enough money?

twelve

we'll meet again

Tick (✓) when you've done these sections.

natural English
- [ ] *me too / me neither*
- [ ] showing surprise
- [ ] greeting old friends

grammar
- [ ] *used to* + verb
- [ ] present perfect and past simple revision
- [ ] expand your grammar short responses

vocabulary
- [ ] activities
- [ ] professions
- [ ] life events
- [ ] expand your vocabulary *see*

 **how to** ... talk about the past

vocabulary activities

1 Mike has decided to use an Internet dating agency. These agencies introduce people with similar interests. He has completed this questionnaire.

Make friends

Tell us about yourself.

You're playing a sport this afternoon. What would you prefer?
- ○ **a** basketball
- ○ **b** tennis
- ◉ **c** golf

1 Do you play any of these instruments? If not, which would you like to learn?
- ○ **a** the piano
- ◉ **b** the guitar
- ○ **c** the violin

2 You're going on holiday. What type of holiday would you prefer?
- ○ **a** skiing
- ○ **b** a beachside resort
- ◉ **c** a sightseeing holiday

3 You're going out with some friends tonight. Where would you like to go?
- ○ **a** the cinema
- ○ **b** a restaurant
- ◉ **c** a club

4 It's your birthday. Which of these activities would you prefer?
- ◉ **a** drinks with friends
- ○ **b** a big party
- ○ **c** dinner with your boyfriend / girlfriend

5 You have a very long train journey. How would you pass the time?
- ◉ **a** cards
- ○ **b** a book
- ○ **c** music

Complete the sentences about Mike. Add words if necessary.

He'd prefer to *play golf.*

1 He'd like to learn how to _____

2 He'd prefer to _____

3 He'd like to _____

4 He'd prefer to _____

5 He'd probably _____

 say it!

Answer the questions in exercise 1 for yourself and then say the sentences.

> I'd prefer to play tennis.

natural English *me too / me neither*

2 Underline the correct words.

   A I work in advertising.
   B <u>Me too.</u> / Me neither.

1 A I don't like flying.
   B Really? I do. / I don't. I love it!

2 A I live in London.
   B Me too. / Me neither. North London.

3 A I go away on business a lot.
   B Really? I do. / I don't. It's my first time.

4 A I've never been to New York before.
   B Me too. / Me neither.

5 A I've got friends in New York.
   B Me too. / Me neither. They live in Manhattan.

grammar *used to + verb*

3 Complete the texts using the verbs in the box with *used to* or in the past simple.

move	make	eat	share	find	~~visit~~
go	work	put	not speak	argue	

Childhood memories

When I was a child we <u>*used to visit*</u> my grandparents in the country nearly every weekend. My granny always ¹_____ her special chocolate cake for us. Once I ²_____ so much of it that I was sick!

My dad ³_____ for an international company and so we ⁴_____ a lot. When I was about ten we ⁵_____ to live in Panama for a year. I remember my first day at school because I ⁶_____ Spanish and couldn't understand anything the teachers said. I learnt it very quickly!

My sister and I ⁷_____ all the time when we were children. She never ⁸_____ her toys with me so one day, when I was about eight years old I ⁹_____ her favourite toy into the rubbish bin. She never ¹⁰_____ the toy and she still reminds me about it now!

write it!

A student magazine has asked students to write about a childhood memory. The best story wins a prize. Write your story.

expand
your grammar

short responses

In exercise 2 you practised saying something <u>isn't true for you</u> using short responses. Here are more examples using different tenses.

past simple

A I <u>didn't</u> like the film.   A I <u>liked</u> the film.
B Really? I <u>did</u>.   B Really? I <u>didn't</u>.

present perfect

A I <u>haven't</u> been   A I<u>'ve</u> been here
   here before.   before.
B Really? I <u>have</u>.   B Really? I <u>haven't</u>.

Complete the sentences saying that this isn't true for you.

   A I've already bought him a present.
   B Really? *I haven't* _____.

1 A I've never been to England.
   B Really? _____.

2 A I passed the test.
   B Really? _____.

3 A I didn't get an invitation to the party.
   B Really? _____.

4 A I've seen this film before.
   B Really? _____.
      Is it good?

5 A I didn't like the food.
   B Really? _____.
      I thought it was great.

wordbooster

professions

think back!

Remember five more professions. *teaching*

4 Make new sentences with the same meanings. Use the words given, changing the form if necessary.

My sister became a nurse. <u>*My sister went into nursing*</u> . (go into)

1 I went into journalism. _____ (become)

2 She became a lawyer. _____ (go into)

3 I want to go into engineering. _____ (become)

4 He wants to become a doctor. _____ (go into)

5 After university I went into banking. _____ (become)

6 My dad became a computer programmer last year. _____ (go into)

7 She'd like to go into business. _____ (become)

8 I'd like to become a teacher. _____ (go into)

life events

5 Nick and Michiko talk about their lives since they left school / university. Order their sentences.

1 I still work in tourism now. I'm the manager of a travel agency.

2 First I spent a year teaching in Spain and then I went to Chile.

3 I spent six months there studying English and travelling.

4 Then we came back to England and got married.

5 That's where I met my wife. She was teaching there too.

6 We stayed in Chile for another year.

7 I worked in the shop for about a year and saved money to go to Australia.

8 ~~I left university in 1991 and became an English teacher.~~

9 When I got home I wanted to use my English so I became a tour guide.

10 ~~After I left school I got a job as a shop assistant in a music store in Tokyo.~~

Nick – England: <u>8</u> , _____ , _____ , _____ , _____ .

Michiko – Japan: <u>10</u> , _____ , _____ , _____ , _____ .

friends reunited

natural English showing surprise

6 Two old friends are talking about people they went to school with several years ago. Complete the responses with sentences a to f.

  A George became a singer.
  B That's incredible! <u>b</u>

1 A Sally became a doctor.
  B I can't believe it. ____

2 A Beth and Luis got married.
  B I don't believe it. ____

3 A Julie's a professional tennis player.
  B That's incredible. ____

4 A Josh went into teaching.
  B Wow! ____

5 A Eddie's a policeman.
  B I can't believe it. ____

a They never used to like each other!

b ~~He used to be so shy.~~

c She used to hate hospitals.

d I used to play against her and win!

e He used to get into trouble all the time.

f He used to hate school.

grammar present perfect and past simple revision

7 Complete the conversation. Use the words in brackets in either the past simple or the present perfect.

Stella How are you?

Olivia Good! It's great to see you again. I _haven't seen_ (not / see) you since we graduated.

Stella I know. What have you been doing?

Olivia Well, I ¹_____ (move) to Melbourne about six months ago for a new job.

Stella What do you do?

Olivia I'm a computer programmer. How about you? What are you doing now?

Stella I work for an advertising company. I ²_____ (work) there since we left college.

Olivia Right.

Stella How long ³_____ (be) in computer programming?

Olivia About two years. I ⁴_____ (spend) a year abroad before that.

Stella Where ⁵_____ (you / go)?

Olivia I worked in England and travelled around Europe a bit.

Stella Sounds great. I'd like to do that.

Olivia Do you still see Paul?

Stella Actually we ⁶_____ (get) married last year.

Olivia Wow! Congratulations! You ⁷_____ (be) together for a long time, haven't you?

Stella About ten years! What about you? Are you married?

Olivia No, no. I've got a boyfriend but we ⁸_____ (not / know) each other for very long.

8 Complete the sentences with a suitable word. Contractions (e.g. *don't*) count as one word.

  A When did they get engaged?

  B _Last_ year.

1 **A** Did you go to the party last night?

  B Yes, I _____ .

2 **A** Have you ever been to America?

  B No, I _____ .

3 **A** How long have you worked there?

  B _____ about five years.

4 **A** When did you two meet?

  B Three years _____ .

5 **A** Have you known each other long?

  B Yes, _____ we were at school.

6 **A** Have you read this book?

  B Yes, I _____ .

7 **A** Did you drive here tonight?

  B No, I _____ .

8 **A** When did you move here?

  B _____ September.

9 **A** Has Charlie arrived yet?

  B No, he _____ .

10 **A** When did you start working here?

  B _____ June 2002.

say it!

Answer these questions about yourself.

> Yes, I have. I've read ...

Have you ever read any books in English?
Have you spoken any English today?
Have you studied any other languages?
Did you have an English lesson last week?
When did you start learning English?

natural English greeting old friends

9 Look at exercise 7 on *p.62* again. Notice the greetings and the questions they ask.

Now order the words to make greetings.

are / how / you
How are you?

1 see / to / it / you / 's / great
A _____
B Yeah, you too.

2 been / have / what / doing / you
A _____ ?
B I've got a new job and I've moved to Melbourne.

3 are / now / you / doing / what
A _____ ?
B I'm studying.

4 a / nurse / long / you / been / how / have
A _____ ?
B For about three years.

5 see / you / still / Andrew / do
A _____ ?
B Yes. We still play squash together every week.

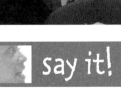

say it!

Think of an old school friend. Imagine that you meet him / her again. Ask five questions.

Hi! It's great to see you again.

expand your vocabulary

see

Read the sentences. Put the phrases with *see* into the correct section of the diagram.

a It's too dark in here. **I can't see** anything.
b Did you know that **Sam is seeing Jemma**?
c Do you want to **see a film** tonight?
d **I'll see if** Tom's busy. Maybe he can help us.
e **I'm seeing Tom** tomorrow. We're going to the cinema.
f A Bye.
  B **See you!**
g A You need to use *since* not *for* in this sentence.
  B **I see.**

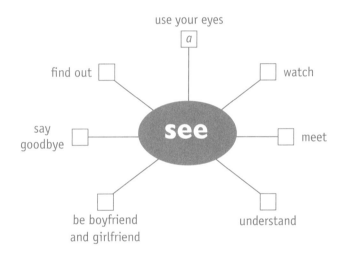

Write new sentences with the same meaning. Use *see*.

I understand.
I see .

1 I watched a great soccer match on Saturday.

_____

2 Is your brother still going out with Sabine?

_____

3 Bye!

_____

4 I met Jessica last night.

_____

5 Can you find out if we've got any coffee?

_____

thirteen

looking for love

Tick (✓) when you've done these sections.

natural English
- [ ] *have (got)* sth *in common*
- [ ] *quite / not very* + adjective
- [ ] asking about people

grammar
- [ ] conditional sentences with *would*
- [ ] defining relative clauses

vocabulary
- [ ] describing character
- [ ] describing appearance

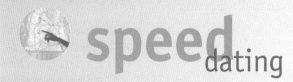

speed dating

natural English *have (got)* sth *in common*

Four university students are thinking of sharing a house together. Look at the information about Joe and Brian. Sentence b is the best way to complete the sentence about them.

Joe and Brian a have got a lot in common.
                  b have got quite a lot in common. ✓
                  c haven't got much in common.

	Steve	**Joe**	**Evan**	**Brian**
sports	soccer, rugby	soccer, tennis	basketball, tennis	tennis, rugby
music	pop	rock, classical	jazz	rock
films	action	action	comedies	comedies
hobbies	reading, computer games	computer games	playing guitar, reading	computer games, playing guitar
food	Italian, Thai	Italian	Indian	Thai
studies	law	law	languages	engineering

1 Now complete these sentences using *have got (quite) a lot / haven't got much in common*.

    Joe and Brian   <u>*have got quite a lot in common.*</u>

  1 Steve and Joe _____

  2 Steve and Brian _____

  3 Steve and Evan _____

  4 Evan and Brian _____

  5 Joe and Evan _____

 say it!

Cover your sentences and look again at the information in the chart. Talk about Steve, Joe, Evan, and Brian, using *have got* sth *in common*.

grammar conditional sentences with *would*

2 Match the questions and answers in this magazine article.

Dream On...

Sarah Carr ACTOR

If money were no problem, what three **luxury items** would you buy? _g_

1 If you could spend a day being someone else, who would it be? ___

2 What's your dream job? ___

3 If you won a trip to the destination of your choice, where would you go? ___

4 What's something you've never done before but would love to try? ___

5 What **talent** would you love to have? ___

6 If you could change one thing about yourself, what would it be? ___

a I would love to try water skiing. It always looks fantastic and I love the water.

b I'd love to be a famous pop star for a day. It would be fun.

c I'd like to be more confident when I'm not acting. Real life is much harder than acting.

d I've always wanted to play the drums well. As a child I had a drum set. It drove my parents crazy but I loved it.

e A tropical island that has only just been discovered. I dream about lying on a beautiful beach with no one else around.

f To be an extremely successful writer. I've always wanted to write novels.

g ~~A big house by the sea, a sports car, and a private plane (with a pilot) so I could travel without booking flights.~~

luxury item /ˈlʌkʃəri/ (adj) /ˈaɪtəm/ (n) something very expensive
talent /ˈtælənt/ (n) something you are naturally very good at

 ## write it!

Write your own answers to the questions for an article in your school magazine.

3 Complete the sentences using the verbs in the past simple or *would* + verb.

A Why don't you look for a new job?
B If I _left_ (leave) now I think it _would be_ (be) difficult to find work.

1 A I think a woman at work is stealing money.
B If I _____ (be) you, I _____ (not say) anything about it. You might be wrong.

2 A I'm going to Paris for the weekend. Why don't you come?
B If I _____ (have) enough money, I _____ (come) with you but I'm saving to buy a car.

3 A I feel awful again today.
B I'm sure you _____ (feel) better if you _____ (go) to bed a bit earlier at night.

4 A What's your new flatmate like?
B I _____ (like) her better if she _____ (not play) loud music all the time.

5 A The train to Glasgow's really expensive.
B It _____ (be) cheaper if you _____ (take) the bus.

6 A Are they going out together?
B If I _____ (know), I _____ (tell) you, but I don't know.

7 A Joon Sung is worried about the exam.
B If he _____ (work) harder, he _____ (get) better results.

8 A Are you going to tell your dad what happened?
B No. If I _____ (tell) him, I'm sure he _____ (get) angry.

wordbooster

describing character

think back!

Remember five adjectives to describe someone's character.

4 Do the crossword.

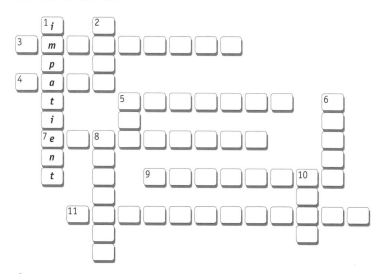

down

1 My mum never gets the bus. She's too ... and hates waiting.

2 She's very ... . She helps everyone.

5 She doesn't like meeting new people – she's a bit ... .

6 I like him – he's very ... . He makes everyone laugh.

8 She's the most ... person I know. She never does anything for anyone else.

10 My brother's very ... . Sometimes at the weekend he stays in bed nearly all day!

across

3 My career is important to me. I'm quite ... .

4 He's very ...-working. Often he works from 7 a.m. to 8 p.m.

5 My dad's quite ... . He doesn't laugh or joke very much.

7 She's very relaxed about things. In fact, she's very ... .

9 My brother's new girlfriend isn't very ... . She didn't smile at all during the party.

11 I can't believe he's not ready for the meeting. He's so ... .

natural English *quite / not very* + adjective

5 Underline the correct word.

I'm sure she wants that job. She's <u>quite</u> / not very ambitious.

1 I'm quite / not very hungry. I think I'll go and get some food.

2 I'm quite / not very tired, so I might stay up and work.

3 I don't want to ask her. She's quite / not very friendly.

4 You'll never make him laugh. He's quite / not very serious.

5 I don't like my job. It's quite / not very boring.

 how to

natural English asking about people

6 Write the questions using *like*.

What does he like doing?

He likes playing tennis and swimming.

1 _____?

He's got dark hair and brown eyes. He's a bit taller than me.

2 _____?

He's quite shy and serious.

3 _____?

She loves playing the guitar and she sings in a band.

4 _____?

She's quite ambitious.

5 _____?

She's very pretty!

say it!

> What does he <u>like</u> doing?

pronunciation Underline the stressed words in the questions in exercise 6. Practise asking them.

Now answer these questions.

What does your boyfriend / girlfriend look like?
What's your teacher like?
What do you like doing?

describe people

Alex _____

1 _____

2 _____

3 _____

4 _____

5 _____

Alex   1   2   3   4   5

vocabulary describing appearance

7 Isabella is a new student. She is talking to Hanna about people at their school. Look at the pictures and write the names.

Hanna   Florence is nice, isn't she?

Isabella Who's Florence?

Hanna   She's in my class. She's got short dark hair. She's pretty. I'm sure you've met her – her boyfriend's called Alex.

Isabella Yeah, I know her, but I don't think I've met Alex. What does he look like?

Hanna   He's got fair hair. He's quite handsome.

Isabella Is he very tall?

Hanna   No, you're thinking of Thomas in my class. Alex is average height and he sometimes wears glasses.

Isabella Oh right. I don't think I've met him yet.

Hanna   What about Carole. Do you know her?

Isabella Maybe. What does she look like?

Hanna   She's got shoulder-length, blonde hair. She's a bit overweight but quite beautiful.

Isabella Oh yeah, I met her today. She was with another girl but I can't remember her name.

Hanna   Melanie?

Isabella I'm not sure.

Hanna   Has she got long, black hair?

Isabella Yes, I think so.

Hanna   That's Melanie. She goes out with Claudio, the Italian guy in your class.

Isabella Claudio? Is he quite short?

Hanna   Yes, that's him.

Isabella He's very good-looking, isn't he?

grammar defining relative clauses

8 Write one new sentence using *who* or *which / that*.

I liked that song.
That song was just on the radio.
I liked that song which was just on the radio.

1 Do you know that girl?
  She's talking to Ben.

  _____

2 That's the teacher.
  He taught us this afternoon.

  _____

3 I saw the new movie.
  It stars Kate Hudson.

  _____

4 Have you met the new neighbours?
  They live across the road.

  _____

5 He works in a shop.
  It sells sports equipment.

  _____

6 We went to that café.
  It's just opened near the cinema.

  _____

7 Did you pick up the dictionary?
  It was on my desk.

  _____

8 The police arrested the man.
  He stole my bag.

  _____

fourteen service with a smile

where shall we stay?

natural English *when / where was that?*

1 Aurea from Brazil is going to travel in New Zealand. She is talking to a friend, Roberto. Put these questions into the conversation below.

a Have you ever stayed in one?
b Was it good?
c When was that?
d ~~Where are you going to stay?~~
e Did you go by yourself?
f Where was that?

Roberto   *Where are you going to stay?*

Aurea   In backpacker hostels. [1]_____ ?

Roberto   Yes.

Aurea   [2]_____ ?

Roberto   In Canada. I studied English there and then went travelling for a month.

Aurea   Did you? [3]_____ ?

Roberto   Last year.

Aurea   [4]_____ ?

Roberto   Yeah. I had a great time.

Aurea   [5]_____ ?

Roberto   No, I was with my best friend.

New Zealand

world travel guides

say it!

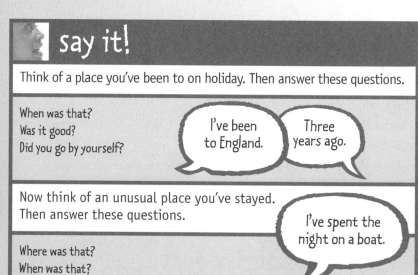

Think of a place you've been to on holiday. Then answer these questions.

When was that?
Was it good?
Did you go by yourself?

> I've been to England.

> Three years ago.

Now think of an unusual place you've stayed. Then answer these questions.

> I've spent the night on a boat.

Where was that?
When was that?

grammar present passives

2 You are going to study at an English college. You receive this information from the college. Underline the correct form.

Your first day at school

When you first arrive, you <u>fill in</u> / are filled in a form with some personal details. Then you ¹ do / are done a written test and you ² interview / are interviewed by one of the teachers. After that the teacher ³ introduces / is introduced all the new students and you ⁴ show / are shown around the college. You ⁵ give / are given a coursebook and a dictionary. After lunch you ⁶ start / are start your new class. Later everyone ⁷ take / is taken on a tour of the city and in the evening you ⁸ invite / are invited to a party.

grammar past passives

3 Complete the letter using the verbs given in the past simple (active or passive).

Dear Sir /Madam,

Last week I ____took____ (take) a flight with your airline from London to Capetown. Unfortunately, the flight ¹_____ (delay) by four hours. We ²_____ (tell) to stay in the departure lounge but no one ³_____ (explain) anything about the delay. We ⁴_____ (offer) a cold drink but no food or hot drinks were available.

Everyone was very hungry when we finally ⁵_____ (get) on the plane but no food ⁶_____ (serve) for the first two hours of the flight. The entertainment was terrible. We ⁷_____ (show) a very old film and my headphones were broken. I ⁸_____ (ask) for some new ones but the air steward never brought me any.

I do not feel this service is good enough for a well-known airline.

I look forward to hearing from you.

Yours faithfully,

Harry Firth.

write it!

Imagine that you went on a one-day sightseeing trip in London. Many things went wrong, e.g. the bus was late; the bus broke down; there was no food. Write a letter of complaint.

wordbooster

hotel rooms and bathrooms

4 Look at the first picture and complete the sentences.

The _toilet paper_____
is on top of the toilet.

1 The _____
is on the edge of the washbasin.

2 The _____
is in the cupboard.

3 The _____
is hanging on the back of the door.

4 The _____
is on the shelf.

5 The _____
is by the window.

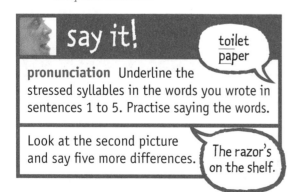

say it!

toilet paper

pronunciation Underline the stressed syllables in the words you wrote in sentences 1 to 5. Practise saying the words.

Look at the second picture and say five more differences.

The razor's on the shelf.

verbs often confused

5 Tick the correct words.

a Could I borrow ✓
b Could I lend
your bike?

1
a I left
b I forgot
my wallet at home.

2 Please don't say
a anything about this.
b anyone about this.

3
a Can I borrow
b Can you lend
me some money?

4 Who told
a you the game was cancelled?
b the game was cancelled?

5
a Did you take
b Did you bring
your camera to Cathy's party last night?

natural English *another/some more*

6 Underline the correct word(s).

A Would you like <u>another</u> / some more glass of wine?

B Yes please.

1 **A** Shall I get you another / some more cup of coffee?
B Yes, I'd love one.

2 **A** Can we have another / some more milk please?
B Yes, of course. Room service will bring some to your room.

3 **A** Can I have another / some more bottle of mineral water please?
B Sure, I'll bring one to your table.

4 **A** Would you like another / some more sandwich?
B No thanks. I'm full.

5 **A** Could we have another / some more bread please?
B Sure, I'll get you some.

6 **A** I'm going to get another / some more chips.
B Me too!

7 **A** Have you got another / some more money?
B How much do we need?

8 **A** Could I have another / some more towel, please?
B Sure.

how to... get through an airport

vocabulary airports

think back!

Remember six more words connected with airports.   *passenger*

7 Match the beginnings and endings of these sentences.

You have to go to terminal   a ten at 10 o'clock.

1 My suitcase is really

2 You are only allowed one piece of hand

3 Could you go straight to the check-in

4 It took a long time to get through passport

5 I can't carry all these bags. Can you get me

6 You should go to the departure

7 Could I possibly have an aisle

8 Could I see your boarding

9 There was a really long queue

10 Go to gate

a ten at 10 o'clock.

b control.

c heavy. I can't pick it up.

d in the café so I didn't wait.

e seat?

f card, please?

g desk?

h luggage.

i one for international flights.

j a trolley?

k lounge now.

test yourself!

Cover the endings on the right. Try to finish the sentences.

natural English requests

8 Complete the sentences using *Could I / you (possibly)* and a word from the box.

| go | help | give | borrow | ~~stay~~ | lend |

Could I possibly stay   with you when I come to Oslo? I arrive on the 17th March.

1 _____ your backpack? I'm going away for the weekend and I've only got a huge suitcase.

2 _____ me some money? I've lost my wallet.

3 _____ me on Saturday? I'm moving house.

4 _____ home early? It's my birthday today.

5 _____ your report to me as soon as possible? I need it for tomorrow's meeting.

natural English taking time to think

9 It is Crystal's first day at a language school in England. Underline three more phrases she uses to take time to think.

teacher   Can you write down your address and phone number?

Crystal   Er, <u>just a moment</u>. I'll have to look for it.

teacher   When did you start learning English?

Crystal   Oh, let me think, I guess I was about 14.

teacher   What do you find easy or difficult in English?

Crystal   Umm, let me see. Well, reading's OK but I don't understand so much when people talk.

teacher   Have you been to England before?

Crystal   Yeah, I studied here last year.

teacher   Which class were you in?

Crystal   I'm not sure. Pre-intermediate I think.

 ## say it!

Answer these questions using a phrase with the word in colour.

> Just a moment, I wrote it down. It was page 55, exercises 7 and 8.

What was the English homework yesterday?
moment

What coursebook do you use in your English class?
minute

When did you start learning English? think

What's your level of English? sure

What do you find easy or difficult in English? see

unit one

1
1 f   5 a
2 b   6 h
3 i   7 g
4 c   8 d

say it!
What's the countryside like?
What's the food like?
What's your town like?
What are the people like?
Students' own answers

eyv
1 a film   a luxurious
2 a hotel   b fun
3 the weather   c scary
4 a party   d spicy
5 a book   e humid
6 a CD   f catchy
7 some food   g popular
8 a teacher   h complicated

2
1 What's your name?
2 Where do you live?
3 What do you do there?
4 Are you on holiday in Italy?
5 Is she Italian?
6 Where did they meet?
7 Have they got any children?
8 How old is he?
9 How often does your brother go back to England?

3 That's interesting!
Really!
Wow!
That's fantastic!

say it! *Students' own answers.*

4
1 I'm an only child.
2 I live on my own.
3 We argue a lot.
4 I get on well with my boss.
5 The teachers at school are very strict.
6 My sister is a single parent.
7 They got married last September.
8 My brother and I are very close.

5
1 brother-in-law
2 niece
3 uncle
4 aunt
5 nephew
6 stepfather
7 cousin
8 daughter

6
1 Loraine's
2 Isabella's
3 Anna's
4 Paul's / Sally's
5 Paul's / Lynda's / Loraine's / Anna's
6 Luke's
7 Lynda's / Loraine's
8 Katie's / Isabella's / Luke's

7
1 started
2 sat
3 talked
4 did
5 got
6 left
7 rented
8 was
9 had
10 moved

8
1 didn't go
2 Did Miki win
3 didn't feel
4 did you leave
5 Did you buy
6 did Sonia go
7 didn't enjoy
8 Did your parents pay

9
1 ✓ true
2 ✓ true
3 ✗ false
4 ✗ false
5 ✗ false

10
1 They both study engineering. / Both of them study engineering.
2 They are both good at art. / Both of them are good at art.
3 They both play the guitar. / Both of them play the guitar.
4 They both hate waiting for things. / Both of them hate waiting for things.
5 They both live in Zurich. / Both of them live in Zurich.

say it! *Students' own answers.*

eyg
1 Neither Simon nor Marcus smokes. / Neither of them smokes.
2 Neither Simon nor Marcus can speak another language. / Neither of them can speak another language.
3 Neither Simon nor Marcus lives at home. / Neither of them lives at home.
4 Neither Simon nor Marcus has a car. / Neither of them has a car.
5 Neither Simon nor Marcus is interested in computers. / Neither of them is interested in computers.

unit two

1
1 I didn't have any breakfast this morning.
2 I have some chocolate every day.
3 Do you want to have lunch with me?
4 We had dinner in a great restaurant.
5 I have had three cups this morning.
6 I had lunch at three o'clock.
7 I am having dinner with my grandparents.
8 Can I have a biscuit?

say it! *Students' own answers.*

2
across   down
1 peppers   3 carrots
5 aubergine   4 grapes
7 olives   6 rice

3
1 e
2 b
3 f
4 a
5 d

4
1 pasta
2 bacon
3 cream
4 cheese
5 fish
6 bread
7 rice
8 water
9 juice

5
1 a lot of
2 many / any
3 much / any
4 much / any
5 a lot of
6 much / any
7 many
8 a lot of

say it! *Students' own answers.*

eyg
1 d
2 b
3 c
4 f
5 a

6
1 i   5 c
2 h   6 e
3 b   7 a
4 f   8 g

7
1 gorgeous
2 delicious
3 brilliant
4 terrible
5 fabulous

say it! *Students' own answers.*

eyv
1 hungry
2 hot
3 tiny
4 exhausted
5 interesting
6 pretty
7 freezing
8 huge / enormous

8 *Sample answers*
1 I'm sorry I'm late. I missed the bus.
2 I'm sorry I'm late. I got lost.
3 I didn't have time to buy any wine. I'm really sorry.
4 I'm sorry I'm late. I had a meeting at work.
5 I didn't have time to buy a present. I'm really sorry.

say it! *Students' own answers*

9
1 kind
2 well
3 easily
4 angry
5 carefully
6 brilliant
7 absolutely
8 incredibly
9 unhappy
10 nicely

10
Don't go to Bluewater Café! I had a ~~terribly~~ *terrible* dinner there last week! We waited for our food for a long time. When it finally came my meal was cold and my friend's meal was disgusting! The waiter was ~~incredible~~ *incredibly* rude and when we complained the manager shouted at us. And the meal was expensive!

Why don't you go to Ceruttis? I had lunch there last Saturday and it was really ~~well~~ *good*. The waitress served us very ~~quick~~ *quickly*. The food was ~~absolute~~ *absolutely* delicious and it was quite ~~cheaply~~ *cheap*. In fact, I'm thinking of going there again next Saturday for my girlfriend's birthday.

unit three

1
1 b
2 e
3 d
4 f
5 a

say it! *Students' own answers.*

2
1 I went
2 I was
3 I've heard
4 I've never been
5 I had
6 Was it
7 Have you met
8 we met
9 didn't you go
10 I finished

3
1 've never met
2 finished
3 got
4 Have you seen
5 Did you go out
6 bought
7 has been
8 've lived

4
1 done a dangerous sport?
2 met a famous person?
3 slept outside?
4 been surfing?
5 climbed a mountain?

say it! *Students' own answers.*

eyg
1 've just bought it.
2 've just seen him.
3 've just finished it.
4 's just had an accident.
5 's just left.

5
1 ugly
2 polluted
3 quiet
4 safe
5 dangerous
6 clean
7 lively
8 peaceful

6
1 It's not far from the train station.
2 It's quite near the hospital.
3 It's a long way from the city centre.
4 Is it far from here?
5 It's quite a long way from my house.

say it! *Students' own answers.*

7
1 a fifty-minute journey
2 a twenty-hour flight
3 a one-hour drive
4 a twelve-week course
5 a two-week tour

8
1 right
2 edge
3 just
4 near
5 corner
6 road
7 close
8 round
9 opposite
10 end

9
1 Where's the nearest bank?
2 How far's the post office?
3 Is there a supermarket near here?
4 How far's the train station?
5 Where's the nearest bus stop?

say it! pronunciation *See ex 9. Students' own answers.*

eyv
1 a	5 c
2 d	6 b
3 f	7 i
4 e	8 h

1 Vancouver Art Gallery
2 shopping centres
3 B.C. Place Stadium
4 Vancouver Museum
5 Vancouver Aquarium
6 information centre
7 Playland Fun Park
8 open-air market

unit four

1 & say it!
1 d
2 e
3 f
4 a
5 b

2
1 He can't afford to buy a car (at the moment).
2 I can't afford to go to the concert.
3 I can't afford to buy new shoes at the moment.
4 We can't afford to stay in a hotel.
5 I can't afford to take a taxi.

3
1 I'll meet
2 I'll send
3 I'll give
4 I'll bring
5 I'll call

write it! *Sample answers*
Sure! I'll have a room ready for you.
I'll bring some pizzas and coke.

eyg
1 Shall
2 Will
3 Shall
4 Will
5 Will

say it!
Will you e-mail me that report tomorrow?
Will you give me that book?
Will you help me with something?
Shall I get you a coffee?
Shall I call you later?
Shall I drive tonight?

4
1 jeans	6 a jacket
2 A skirt	7 a tie
3 a top	8 high heels
4 a suit	9 trainers
5 a shirt	10 a jumper

5
1 C	5 W
2 C	6 W
3 W	7 C
4 W	8 W

say it!
handbag	bracelet
umbrella	briefcase
make-up	necklace
glasses	

Do you usually carry a briefcase, a handbag, or a backpack?
Do you often wear jewellery? What kind?
Do you have to wear glasses or contact lenses?

6
1 try them on
2 pick them up
3 take it back
4 turn it off
5 put it down

7
1 size
2 bigger
3 counter
4 changing
5 fit

8
c Can I ~~try on them~~ *try them on* please?
sa What size are you?
c 39, I think.
sa We haven't got any in 39 but you can try 38½.
c OK … No, they ~~doesn't~~ *don't* fit. They ~~is~~ *are* a bit small.
sa How's the shirt?
c It's ~~a~~ *the* wrong size. It ~~be~~ *is* too tight.
sa What ~~are you size~~ *size are you*?
c I'm usually *a* ten.
sa OK, if the ten's too small I'll look for a twelve.
sa How's that one?
c Much better.
sa It ~~look~~ *looks* good on you. It's a great colour.
c It's nice, isn't it? Where *do* I pay?

9
1 is too expensive
2 's too far
3 're too late
4 is too difficult
5 'm too tired
6 's too cold
7 's too dark
8 's too young

10
1 very
2 very
3 too
4 very
5 too

11
1 too much sugar
2 too many words
3 too much money
4 too many students
5 too many people

say it!
We've ordered too much food.
No. I've got too much work to do.
That bag's got too many books in it.

eyv
1 pay by
2 cost $25
3 buy
4 price
5 paid $100
6 buy you
7 pay for
8 cost

unit five

1
1	i	5	h
2	e	6	c
3	f	7	g
4	a	8	d

say it! *Students' own answers.*

2
1 bookshelf
2 computer
3 cassette
4 file
5 video
6 cassette recorder
7 headphones
8 photocopier

```
C  C (B  O  O  T  T  P  F (H) A
(P (H  O  T  O  C  O  P  I  E  R)
Y  U  O  M  I (V) I  R  L  A  E
B  O  K  J  P (F  I  L  E) D  C
C  A  S  S  E  U  C  D  K  P  O
H  B  H  E  A  D  T  N  E  H  P
W  P  E (C  O  M  P  E  R  O) H
F  I  L  T  D  T  F  G  R  N  O
M  H  F (R  E  C  O  R  D  E  R)
(C  A  S  S  E  T  T  E) L (S) E
```

3
1 don't have to
2 can't
3 don't have to
4 have to
5 have to
6 can't
7 don't have to
8 can't

4
1 had to be
2 do you have to start
3 didn't have to go
4 Did you have to wear
5 had / have to buy
6 don't have to work
7 has to look after
8 doesn't have to come
9 had to get
10 Does he have to speak

eyg
1 I've got to study tonight.
2 Have you got to work this weekend?
3 She's got to help her sister.
4 You've got to be there at 8 p.m.
5 We've got to leave now.

5
1 Can I have a shower? b
2 Is it OK if I make a coffee? e
3 Can I turn on the TV? a
4 Is it OK if I check my e-mails? c
5 Is it OK if I use the washing machine? d

say it!
Can I / Is it OK if I close the window?
Can I / Is it OK if I turn on the radio?
Can I / Is it OK if I use the microwave?

think back!
primary school (eight)
secondary school (fourteen)
university (twenty)

6
1 joined
2 pass
3 wear
4 missed
5 left
6 go
7 revise
8 take

eyv
1	e	5	b
2	h	6	i
3	c	7	a
4	g	8	d

say it! *Students' own answers.*

7
1 what I like
2 when I like
3 when we like
4 when you like
5 what I like

8 & say it!
1 I <u>think</u> that's <u>true</u>.
2 That's <u>right</u>.
3 I <u>don't</u> think that's <u>true</u>.
4 I'm not <u>sure</u> about that.
5 It dep<u>ends</u>.

9
1 e
2 d
3 b
4 f
5 a

unit six

1 & say it!
1 Byron Bay
2 Cairns
3 Perth
4 Melbourne
5 Alice Springs
6 Darwin
7 Byron Bay
8 Tasmania

2
1 ✓
2 ✗ largest
3 ✗ the
4 ✓
5 ✗ driest
6 ✓
7 ✗ most poisonous
8 ✗ best

3
1 the cleverest
2 the most exciting
3 the most popular
4 the worst
5 the most beautiful
6 the youngest
7 the best
8 the most important

eyv
1	a	5	f
2	h	6	g
3	e	7	d
4	c	8	i

eyg
1 Maria Carmen comes from ~~the~~ South America.
2 He lives near ~~the~~ Independence Square.
3 ✓
4 Have you been to ~~the~~ Cairo?
5 We stayed in a hotel on ~~the~~ Lake Louise.
6 I've been to ~~the~~ Mount Kilimanjaro.
7 ✓
8 We went to Disneyland in ~~the~~ Florida.
9 ✓
10 ✓

4
1 more expensive
2 smaller
3 more comfortable
4 livelier
5 more relaxed
6 younger
7 cheaper
8 better

say it!
The East Coast trip has a bigger group of people.
The East Coast trip is longer.
The Travel North trip is more comfortable.
The Travel North trip is more expensive.

think back!
1 sunshine / sunny
2 snow
3 wind / windy
4 rain
5 cloud / cloudy
6 fog / foggy

5
1 snow
2 windy
3 rain
4 sunny
5 cloudy

6 graph 1 c (Alice Springs)
graph 2 a (Darwin)
graph 3 b (Hobart)

7
1 ✓
2 ✓
3 We had a bit of rain.
4 ✓
5 I've got a bit of money.

8
1	e	c	1
2	a	b	2
3	c	e	3
4	f	a	4
5	d	f	5

say it! *Students' own answers.*

9
1 thinks they'll get married / thinks they're going to get married
2 'm sure there won't be / 'm sure there aren't going to be
3 'll probably be / 's probably going to be
4 don't think it'll rain / don't think it's going to rain
5 'm sure you'll enjoy / 'm sure you're going to enjoy
6 do you think you'll be / do you think you're going to be
7 'll probably give / 're probably going to give
8 doesn't think she'll pass / doesn't think she's going to pass
9 think I'll get / think I'm going to get
10 Are you sure you'll be / Are you sure you're going to be

10
1 half an hour or so
2 about 100km
3 around 6 o'clock
4 a week or so
5 about 1.8m
6 around 30 years
7 about $50
8 around 50 people

unit seven

1
1 Do you want to go *and* see a film tonight?
2 She's gone *to* the cinema.
3 I usually go *for* a run in the mornings.
4 ✓
5 Are you going *to* Soraya's party on Friday?
6 I have to go *and* buy a birthday present for my brother.
7 ✓
8 Shall we go *for* a meal before the film tonight?

say it!
I'm going swimming.
I have to go and see a friend.
I usually go for a walk in the morning.
I went to a wedding.

2 then
Afterwards
First
After that
Then

3
a 5   a ✓ started ... ✗ bit
b 6   b ✗ threw
c 4   c ✓ fell ... ✗ hurt
d 1   d ✗ was
e 3   e ✗ ran
f 8   f ✓ got ... ✗ broke
g 7   g ✗ caught
h 2   h ✗ stole ... ✓ rushed

say it!
a started ... bitten
b thrown
c fallen ... hurt
d been
e run
f got ... broken
g caught
h stolen ... rushed

4
1 h   5 a
2 d   6 i
3 b   7 e
4 f   8 g

eyv
1 punch
2 attack
3 grab
4 sprint
5 chuck
6 yell
7 chase
8 smash

5
1 No, we had a terrible time.
2 She's not having a good time.
3 Did you have a good time?
4 Why? I'm having a great time.
5 Have a good time.
6 No, he didn't have a good time.
7 I had a great time.
8 Are you having a good time?

say it!
I had a great time.
Did you have a good time?
Have a good time.
He wasn't having a good time.

6
1 my e-mail
2 the cinema
3 a high mark
4 London
5 work
6 a prize
7 a CD player
8 here

7
1 was walking
2 dropped
3 fell
4 helped
5 was sitting
6 arrived
7 was wearing
8 got
9 met
10 were studying

say it! *Student's own answers.*

8
1 We met when I was living in France.
2 I was driving home when my car broke down.
3 I saw her when I was walking to work.
4 I was doing my homework when Frederick turned up.
5 What were you doing when I phoned you this morning?
6 I burnt / burned my hand when I was cooking dinner.
7 We were travelling in India when my sister got sick.
8 I fell over when I was running for the bus.

9 What's this called in English?
How do you say *ladrillo* in English?

1 a helicopter
2 a pilot
3 a picnic
4 a fire alarm
5 a shoulder

say it! *Students' own answers.*

eyg
1 were making ... were doing
2 was making ... were driving
3 were talking ... was watching
4 was living ... was doing
5 Were you listening ... was talking
6 were you doing ... was working
7 was going out with ... was seeing
8 were having ... was trying

unit eight

1
1 What about going to a club?
2 You could have a picnic in the park.
3 How about getting tickets for a show?
4 How about going out for a meal?
5 What about going away for the weekend?

say it!
How / *What* about going *swimming* / *to the swimming pool?* / *We could go swimming* / *to the swimming pool.*
How / *What* about going for a walk? / We could go for a walk.
How / *What* about going shopping? / We could go shopping.

2
1 a
2 b
3 a
4 a
5 b

3
1 'm going to work
2 'd like to have
3 might go
4 'd like to go
5 are going to stay

4
1 e   5 a
2 i   6 f
3 d   7 g
4 h   8 b

say it!
b last Thursday / four days ago
c the day before yesterday / two days ago
d the day after tomorrow / in two days' time
e this / next Sunday / in six days' time
f in ten days' time

eyv
1 a lie-in
2 an early night
3 a family get-together
4 a night out
5 a very busy day
6 a late night
7 a night in
8 a quiet day

1 have a night out
2 have a family get-together
3 have a lie-in
4 have a rest
5 have an early night
6 have a busy day
7 have a night in
8 had a quiet day

5
1 Yoshiaki had to work all night.
2 It rained all week.
3 I have to study all day on Saturday.
4 I feel tired all the time.
5 She was in the meeting all day.

think back!
accept an invitation
make a booking / arrangements / an appointment / plans
invite friends for dinner
refuse an invitation
book a table

6
1a accept the invitation
1b made ... plans
1c refuse the invitation
2a (invite ... party)
3a made a dentist's appointment
4a invite them for dinner
4b book a table
5a made arrangements

7
1 you want to play
2 you like to *come* / *go*
3 you want to *come* / *go*
4 you like to have
5 you want to *come* / *go*

1 'd love to.
2 I can't.

say it!
Do you want to *come* / *go* to a concert? / Would you like to *come* / *go* to a concert?
Do you want to *come* / *go* to the beach? / Would you like to *come* / *go* to the beach?
Do you want to *rent* / *watch* a DVD? / Would you like to *rent* / *watch* a DVD?
Do you want to have lunch? / Would you like to have lunch?

8
1 a
2 c
3 b
4 d
5 e

9
1 I'm not doing anything tomorrow night.
2 Are you coming to the concert next Friday?
3 I'm playing volleyball this afternoon.
4 We're meeting at 6 o'clock.
5 My parents are having a dinner party tonight.
6 What are you doing this weekend?
7 My sister is staying at a friend's house all weekend.
8 Where are you having dinner?

eyg
1 does the concert start?
2 are you meeting
3 finishes
4 'm having
5 is
6 goes
7 're going
8 begins

unit nine

1
1 Do you still work in advertising?
2 Do you still play a lot of tennis?
3 Are you still friends with Chloe?
4 Does your brother still sing in a band?
5 Are you still going out with Charlie?

2
1 I still live with my parents.
2 I am still at university.
3 My sister still lives in Spain.
4 I still want to be a writer.
5 I am still friends with Vanessa.

say it!
1 Do you still live with your parents?
2 Are you still at university?
3 Does your sister still live in Spain?
4 Do you still want to be a writer?
5 Are you still friends with Vanessa?

3
1 a and c
2 a
3 a and b
4 a and b
5 b

4
1 haven't seen
2 do you live
3 moved
4 work
5 've been
6 Do you still work
7 've been
8 've known

5
1 f   5 g
2 a   6 c
3 e   7 b
4 i   8 h

6 *across:*
1 dining room
3 bathroom
5 landing
8 toilet
9 patio

down:
2 ground floor
3 balcony
4 hall
6 garage
7 stairs

7
1 ~~light~~ dark
2 ~~tidy~~ untidy
3 ~~traditional~~ modern
4 ~~small~~ spacious
5 ~~warm~~ cold

8 *Healthworks*
1 's got a sauna.
2 's a gym.
3 hasn't got a yoga studio.
4 are two cafés.
5 hasn't got a car park.

Fitness One
1 it got a sauna? No, it hasn't.
2 there a gym? Yes, there is.
3 it got a yoga studio? Yes, it has.
4 there a café? No, there isn't.
5 it got a car park? No, it hasn't.

say it!
Solo Gym
There's a sauna. / It's got a sauna.
There's a gym. / It's got a gym.
It hasn't got a yoga studio.
There's a café. / It's got a café.
There are two car parks. / It's got two car parks.

eyv
1 keyring
2 front door
3 kitchen cupboard
4 light switch
5 armchair
6 video camera
7 computer desk
8 fireplace

9
1 should
2 should
3 shouldn't
4 shouldn't
5 should

say it!
You should take a taxi and arrive on time.
You shouldn't talk too much.
You should take your CV with you.
+ *Students' own answers.*

10
1 a
2 c
3 b
4 d
5 e

eyg
1 anybody
2 everything
3 somebody
4 anything
5 Nobody
6 somewhere
7 Everybody
8 anywhere

unit ten

1
1 What time do you usually go **to** bed?
2 Do you find it difficult to **fall** asleep?
3 Do you talk **in** your sleep?
4 Do noises in the night wake **you** up easily?
5 Do you ever **have** nightmares?

a 5
b 2
c *example*
d 1
e 4
f 3

say it! *Students' own answers.*

2 & say it!
1 was *very / really* em<u>barr</u>assed.
5 was *very / really* <u>int</u>eresting.
2 was *very / really* <u>bor</u>ing.
6 was *very / really* <u>fright</u>ening.
3 's *very / really* ex<u>cit</u>ed.
7 was *very / really* sur<u>prised</u>.
4 's *very / really* <u>worr</u>ied.
8 was *very / really* re<u>lax</u>ing.

3
1 c
2 a
3 b

4
1 **A** What's the matter?
  B My arm hurts.
2 **A** What's wrong?
  B I've got a terrible pain in my foot.
3 **A** I feel sick.
  B Would you like some water?
4 **A** I've got a headache.
  B I'll get you some tablets.
5 **A** I don't feel well.
  B Why don't you go home?

say it!
I've got a <u>pain</u> in my <u>leg</u>.
My <u>back</u> hurts.
I've got <u>tooth</u>ache.
I feel <u>sick</u>.

eyv
1 a   1 a plaster
2 c   2 in bed
3 b   3 tissues
4 e   4 cream

5
1 ✗ Don't forget to phone ~~to~~ your dad.
2 ✗ Did you thank ~~to~~ Justyna for the present?
3 ✓
4 ✗ Did you e-mail ~~to~~ Louise?
5 ✗ I sent ~~to~~ him a text message.
6 ✓
7 ✗ Why didn't you ask ~~to~~ me?
8 ✗ I didn't tell ~~to~~ Aidan anything.

6
1 I have to e-mail Pedro.
2 I have to phone the doctor.
3 I have to speak to Barbara.
4 I have to thank Sid for the flowers.
5 I have to talk to Pierre.
6 I have to ring Delphine.
7 I have to ask Fiona for her class notes.
8 I have to send a text message to Mirko.

7
1 I'm afraid I can't.
2 How about Tuesday?
3 That's great.
4 I'm sorry that's no good.
5 That's fine.

say it! *Sample answers*
a I'm afraid I can't.
  That would be great.
b I'm sorry that's no good.
  That's fine. / That's great.

8
1 Well, I've got really bad stomachache.
2 Hmmm, for about three days.
3 Just here.
4 Let me see, er, I had some toast for breakfast. That's all.
5 No, never.
  Hmmm, Now, Right, Let me see

eyg
1 'd better / should
2 should
3 'd better / should
4 had better / should
5 should

1 'd better go to the dentist.
2 'd better phone her.
3 'd better buy tickets today.
4 'd better look again.
5 'd better set my alarm clock.

unit eleven

1 1 Need some help?
2 Hungry?
3 Don't think so.
4 Have a good time? / Good time?
5 Got any change?
6 OK?
7 Like a coffee? / A coffee? / Coffee?
8 Tell you later.

1 Hungry?
2 OK?
3 Like a coffee?
4 Have a good time?
5 Don't think so.
6 Need some help?
7 Got any change?
8 Tell you later.

say it!
Tired?
Been here long?
Got any paper?
Call you tonight.
See you later.

eyg
1 She wasn't upset about it but he was.
2 I wanted to go home but my friends didn't.
3 I still live at home but my sister doesn't.
4 David didn't like the film but I did.
5 She's French but he isn't.
6 Meg doesn't work on Saturdays but Chris does.
7 My flatmate can cook but I can't.
8 Jessica doesn't like him but I do.
9 My dad's excited about it but my mum isn't.
10 I didn't go to the concert but Nadine did.

2 1 b
2 a
3 c

3 1 run
2 working hours
3 to
4 salary
5 work
6 lunch break
7 share
8 get

4 1 a
2 c
3 b
4 f
5 e

say it! *Students' own answers.*

eyv
1 scanner
2 menu
3 monitor
4 icon
5 toolbar
6 screen
7 keyboard
8 disk drive
9 mouse
10 printer

5 & say it!
1 personnel manager
2 receptionist
3 secretary
4 accountant
5 sales manager

6 1 argument
2 split
3 good
4 lazy
5 upset
6 afraid
7 out
8 fell

7 1 'll get
2 won't have to work
3 go
4 'll have to make
5 stay
6 might become
7 become
8 'll earn

8 1 'll do … have
2 leave … 'll look
3 won't wait … 're
4 'll call … needs
5 talk … 'll / might listen
6 'll lose … does
7 'll text … get
8 don't leave … 'll miss

9 1 What if I fail the exam?
2 What if he doesn't like the CD?
3 What if they're late?
4 What if I don't like the job?
5 What if you forget to give him the message?

say it!
What if you don't get a job?
What if you don't like it there?
What if you're lonely?
What if you don't find a place to live?

unit twelve

1 1 play the guitar.
2 go sightseeing. / go on a sightseeing holiday.
3 go to a club.
4 have drinks with friends. / go (out) for drinks with friends.
5 play cards.

say it! *Students' own answers.*

2 1 I do.
2 Me too.
3 I don't.
4 Me neither.
5 Me too.

3 1 used to make
2 ate
3 used to work
4 used to move
5 went
6 didn't speak
7 used to argue
8 used to share
9 put
10 found

eyg
1 I have.
2 I didn't.
3 I did.
4 I haven't.
5 I did.

4 1 I became a journalist.
2 She went into law.
3 I want to become an engineer.
4 He wants to go into medicine.
5 After university I became a banker.
6 My dad went into computer programming last year.
7 She'd like to become a businesswoman.
8 I'd like to go into teaching.

5 Nick (English) Michiko (Japanese)
8	10
2	7
5	3
6	9
4	1

6 1 c
2 a
3 d
4 f
5 e

7 1 moved
2 've worked
3 have you been
4 spent
5 did you go
6 got
7 've been
8 haven't known

8 1 did.
2 haven't.
3 For
4 ago.
5 since
6 have.
7 didn't.
8 Last / In
9 hasn't.
10 In

say it! *Students' own answers.*

9 1 It's great to see you.
2 What have you been doing?
3 What are you doing now?
4 How long have you been a nurse?
5 Do you still see Andrew?

say it! *Students' own answers.*

eyv
watch c
meet e
understand g
be boyfriend and girlfriend b
say goodbye f
find out d

1 I saw a great soccer match on Saturday.
2 Is your brother still seeing Sabine?
3 See you!
4 I saw Jessica last night.
5 Can you see if we've got any coffee?

unit thirteen

1 & say it!
1 have got a lot in common.
2 have got quite a lot in common.
3 haven't got much in common.
4 have got quite a lot in common.
5 haven't got much in common.

2 1 b
2 f
3 e
4 a
5 d
6 c

3 1 was / were … wouldn't say
2 had … would ('d) come
3 would ('d) feel … went
4 would ('d) like … didn't play
5 would ('d) be … took
6 knew … would ('d) tell
7 worked … would ('d) get
8 told … would ('d) get

4 *across*
3 ambitious
4 hard
5 serious
7 easy-going
9 friendly
11 disorganized

down
1 impatient
2 kind
5 shy
6 funny
8 selfish
10 lazy

5 1 quite
2 not very
3 not very
4 quite
5 quite

6 & say it!
1 <u>What</u> does he <u>look</u> like?
2 <u>What</u>'s he <u>like</u>?
3 <u>What</u> does she <u>like doing</u>?
4 <u>What</u>'s she <u>like</u>?
5 <u>What</u> does she <u>look</u> like?

Students' own answers.

7 1 Claudio
2 Thomas
3 Melanie
4 Florence
5 Carole

8 1 Do you know that girl who is talking to Ben?
2 That's the teacher who taught us this afternoon.
3 I saw the new movie *which / that* stars Kate Hudson.
4 Have you met the new neighbours who live across the road?
5 He works in a shop *which / that* sells sports equipment.
6 We went to that café *which / that* has just opened near the cinema.
7 Did you pick up the dictionary *which / that* was on my desk?
8 The police arrested the man who stole my bag.

unit fourteen

1 1 a
2 f
3 c
4 b
5 e

say it! *Students' own answers.*

2 1 do
2 are interviewed
3 introduces
4 are shown
5 are given
6 start
7 is taken
8 are invited

3 1 was delayed
2 were told
3 explained
4 were offered
5 got
6 was served
7 were shown
8 asked

4 & say it!
1 <u>ra</u>zor
2 <u>tooth</u>paste
3 <u>tow</u>el
4 <u>hair</u>dryer
5 soap

The toilet paper's on the floor.
The toothpaste's by the window.
The towel's on the (edge of the) bath.
The hairdryer's in the cupboard.
The soap's on the (edge of the) washbasin.

5 1 a
2 a
3 b
4 a
5 a

6 1 another
2 some more
3 another
4 another
5 some more
6 some more
7 some more
8 another

7 1 c   6 k
2 h   7 e
3 g   8 f
4 b   9 d
5 j   10 a

8 1 Could I (possibly) borrow
2 Could you (possibly) lend
3 Could you (possibly) help
4 Could I (possibly) go
5 Could you (possibly) give

9 let me think
let me see
I'm not sure

say it!
Just a minute …
Let me think …
I'm not sure …
Let me see …
+ *Students' own answers.*

OXFORD
UNIVERSITY PRESS

Great Clarendon Street, Oxford OX2 6DP

Oxford University Press is a department of the University of Oxford.
It furthers the University's objective of excellence in research, scholarship,
and education by publishing worldwide in

Oxford New York

Auckland Cape Town Dar es Salaam Hong Kong Karachi
Kuala Lumpur Madrid Melbourne Mexico City Nairobi
New Delhi Shanghai Taipei Toronto

With offices in

Argentina Austria Brazil Chile Czech Republic France Greece
Guatemala Hungary Italy Japan Poland Portugal Singapore
South Korea Switzerland Thailand Turkey Ukraine Vietnam

OXFORD and OXFORD ENGLISH are registered trade marks of
Oxford University Press in the UK and in certain other countries

© Oxford University Press 2005

The moral rights of the author have been asserted

Database right Oxford University Press (maker)

First published 2005

2009 2008 2007 2006 2005
10 9 8 7 6 5 4 3 2 1

ISBN-13: 978 0 19 438864 1
ISBN-10: 0 19 438864 6

Printed in China

ACKNOWLEDGEMENTS

Designed by: Bryony Newhouse

Although every effort has been made to trace and contact copyright holders
before publication, this has not been possible in some cases. We apologize
for any apparent infringement of copyright and if notified, the publisher will
be pleased to rectify any errors or omissions at the earliest opportunity.

Illustrations: Mark Duffin pp.29, 56; Martina Farrow pp.25, 19, 27, 39, 42, 60;
Phil Healey pp.32, 38; Joanna Kerr pp.10, 11, 21, 25, 38 (objects), 46, 47, 70;
Belle Mellor pp.12, 65; Paul Oakley p.51; Gavin Reece pp.9, 34, 35, 55, 67.

*The Publisher and Authors would also like to thank the following for permission to
reproduce photographs*: Alamy pp.10 (older woman / John Phillips / Photofusion
Picture Library), 13 (outside café / Paul Panayiotou), 37 (Charlotte and Pascal /
plainpicture / Läpple, K.), 37 (Rachael and Jason / plainpicture / Timm, N.),
43 (Andy Bishop); Corbis UK Ltd pp.4 (Larry Lee Photography), 5 (Julian
Hirshowitz), 6 (Jose Luis Pelaez, Inc.), 8 (Rick Gomez), 10 (Japanese girl /
Leland Bobbè), 11 (Jon Feingersh), 14 (woman on sofa / Joyce Choo), 14 (man /
Tom & Dee Ann McCarthy), 17 (building / Adam Woolfitt), 17 (living room /
Graham Henderson / Elizabeth Whiting & Associates), 18 (Ron Watts),
24 (Michael Keller), 28 (David Raymer), 29 (L. Clarke), 30 (Brandon D. Cole),
30 (Martin Harvey), 30 (Freelance Consulting Services Pty Ltd), 33 (Paul A.
Souders), 35 (Firefly Productions), 39 (Steve Prezant), 45 (Michael Prince),
49 (Laureen March), 50 (teacher / Layne Kennedy), 50 (hiker / Lawrence
Manning), 56 (gym / Helen King), 56 (man / Laureen March), 61 (woman /
Randy Faris), 61 (man / Philip Harvey), 62 (© LWA-Stephen Welstead),
63 (Chuck Savage), 66 (Mark A. Johnson), 68 (book / Photowood Inc.);
Education Photos p.7; Getty Images cover and p.1 (Uwe Krejci / two people),
pp.13 (inside restaurant / AJA Productions), 16 (Mike Brinson / The Image
Bank), 21 (Ron Chapple / Taxi), 44 (David C Ellis / Taxi), 47 (David Woolley /
Stone), 50 (skiier / Ryan McVay / The Image Bank), 54 (Jon Feingersh / The
Image Bank), 57 (Ghislain & Marie David de Lossy / The Image Bank),
64 (Stewart Cohen / Taxi), 69 (man on plane / Sean Murphy / Stone); Oxford
University Press p.71; Photodisc all circular and square icon images throughout;
Powerstock Superstock pp.14 (nurse / Javier Larrea / age fotostock), 37 (Marta
and Jakub / Teresa Ponseti / age fotostock), 40 (Javier Larrea / age fotostock),
41 (Jaume Gual / age fotostock), 52 (Michael N. Paras / age fotostock),
59 (Fabio Cardoso / age fotostock), 68 (girl / Javier Larrea / age fotostock);
Science Photo Library p.53; St. Clare's, Oxford pp.25, 69 (girl by door);
Zooid Pictures p.48.